CALLING ALL QUIRKY QUILTERS!

Do you love quilts but yearn to make something a little out of the ordinary? Do you gravitate toward nontraditional materials—think T-shirts, blue jeans, and faux fur—and offbeat techniques? Then you're a certified Quirky Quilter and we think you'll enjoy the unusual patterns in this book.

Here you will find unexpected designs and techniques to spark your interest, whether you're an experienced quilter or just starting out. Even if you're a complete beginner, you can jump right in with Not Your Usual T-shirt Quilt, From Scraps to Stitches Pillow, or Wacky Tacky Bag. Each can be made in an afternoon.

If you're a more experienced quilter, try your hand at the innovative techniques presented in Mum's the Word, which uses fabric paint and a self-made stamp to create a lovely wall hanging, or Mini Masterpiece, which uses photo transfer methods that turn a child's drawing into fine art.

Vintage neckties, time-worn blue jeans and T-shirts, antique quilt scraps, and unusual buttons are among the idiosyncratic materials used in these projects. The All Tied Up chapter offers tips for sewing with neckties, and patterns for two halter tops and a kicky shoulder bag with beaded fringe. Using the Shoo-Fly Rag Throw and From Scraps to Stitches Pillow patterns, you can turn your old blue jeans into a warm, soft throw and coordinating pillow. Or, in Cirque de Fabrique, make an unusual wall hanging with a circus feel using fabric scraps from old clothes and other sewing projects.

Feeling arty? Set a dinner table fit for Frank Lloyd Wright with the Dinner Is Served Table Runner and Placemats. Or try a quilted alternative to standard greeting cards: the Let's Celebrate! card, made from fabric and beads. You can even take quilting to the gym with the Lotus Blossom Yoga Bag.

Whatever your mood or skill level, you're bound to find a project you just *have* to make. We've included lots of useful techniques and tips to get you started, answers to some common quilting questions, and tips to help you finish and display your projects with panache.

Here's wishing you many "pieceful" hours of quilting, from one quirky quilter to another.

Tomme J. Fent

HOW TO BE A QUIRKY QUILTER

The following techniques and tips will help you achieve the best results when you tackle the projects in this book. This information doesn't attempt to compete with the many comprehensive quilting-technique books that are already available. We're making some basic assumptions about you and your abilities. Yes, we're aware of what can happen when we assume something, but we've chosen to prioritize fun and dedicate most of the space in this book to the projects. So we're going out on a limb and assuming the following about you:

- You have a sewing machine that will sew straight and zigzag stitches.
- You actually know how to *use* the sewing machine.

- You maintain your sewing machine reasonably well. This means you clean out the bobbin area more than once a year (every time you change the bobbin is best); keep the machine oiled, if required, per the manufacturer's instructions; and generally keep things in good repair.
- You have a supply of new, sharp needles for both machine and hand sewing.
- You have basic sewing tools and notions, like scissors (for fabric and paper), straight pins (glass heads are great—they won't melt when you iron over them), a seam ripper, a seam gauge or small ruler, an iron, and an ironing board or other padded surface.

In addition, you may find the following information about tools and techniques helpful. Pick and choose what you need to read about, depending on your skill level.

must-have tools

CUTTING TOOLS

The biggest must-have tools for quilters are the rotary cutter, ruler, and mat.

- **Rotary cutter.** These come in a variety of styles and sizes. For general cutting like you'll find in these projects, we recommend a 60-mm rotary cutter, which will handle everything from heavy denim to lightweight rayon with equal ease. For cutting curves, like the wavy border in Hearts Afire, and appliqué shapes, an 18-mm rotary cutter makes the job easier. Keep a few new blades handy too.

do it right: Rotary blades are extremely sharp. Always cut by pushing the blade away from your body, not pulling it toward you. Make it a habit to close your rotary cutter each time you lay it down, even if it's only for a moment, and never leave a rotary cutter or blades within reach of children. Dispose of blades in a safe container, such as the case from the replacement blade.

- **Rotary cutting mat.** A rotary cutter is used with a special self-healing mat. We suggest getting the biggest that you can afford and find room for in your sewing area. We're waiting for someone to come out with a mat the size of a dining room table, but for starters, a mat that's at least 17" x 23" will do.
- **Rulers.** You'll also need a heavy acrylic ruler made for use with rotary cutters. The most-used ruler is 24" long and either 6" or 6½" wide. (A 6½"-wide ruler is great for making 6" blocks.) Choose a ruler that has markings at least every ⅛". Another often-used ruler is a square, in 12" or 15" size. Smaller squares are also useful, as are 45° and 60° triangles (required for the Makin' Me Dizzy Quilt). There are even rotary rulers available to cut interesting shapes, like the Wave-Edge™ Ruler used to make the wavy borders for the Hearts Afire Quilt. Rulers may be stored conveniently on a pegboard or in a slotted ruler holder.
- **Snips.** A labor-saving cutting tool is a pair of spring-action snips. These speed up and ease the process of clipping the exposed seams on rag quilts and throws, such as the Shoo-Fly Rag Throw.

MARKING TOOLS

In many cases, you'll find you need to make temporary markings on fabric to use as stitching or quilting guides. At other times, you may want to make permanent markings, for instance to add your signature to a block for a quilting exchange. For **temporary markings**, we like water-soluble markers for medium to light fabrics, and either a silver pencil, white soapstone, or white chalk marker for very dark fabrics. You can also use a graphite or lead pencil when the markings won't show (as when you're making half-square triangles from squares), and

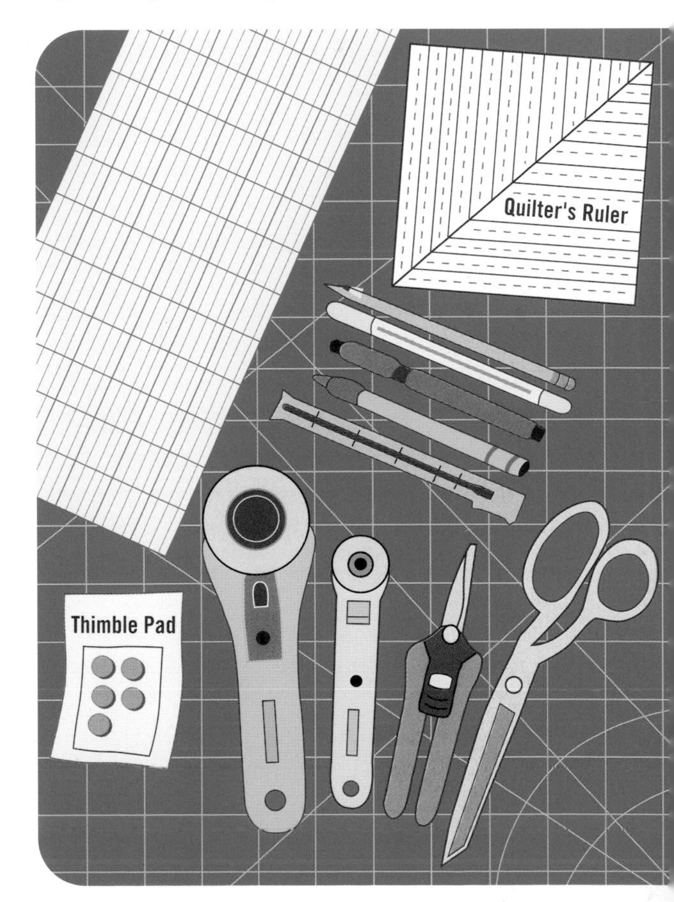

sometimes you even can use masking tape and sew along the edge, removing the tape when you're finished sewing.

do it right: Before using any water-soluble or "disappearing" fabric marker, be sure to test the marker on a scrap of your fabric, following the manufacturer's directions. The fiber content and weave of some fabrics will keep the marks from disappearing, and some markers may leave stains on certain types of fabric.

quilt wise

To keep the blue markings made by "disappearing" markers from reappearing, add a teaspoon of baking soda to a spray bottle of water and wet the marks thoroughly. Allow to dry completely before washing. Note that the baking soda solution must be fresh.

For **permanent markings**, we always keep a variety of colors of permanent pens and fabric markers on hand. Use these to make labels, add pen stitching, touch up peekaboo threads, and add details to appliqués. Choose pens that use archival, colorfast inks and are proven to work well on fabrics. Many of the ink pens and gel pens used in scrapbooking also work well on fabric.

OTHER USEFUL TOOLS

There are a few other doodads we can't live without. We're not being paid to advertise these products, or the other products mentioned by name in this book. We just think they're the best products available for the jobs they do. These products are available through your local quilt shop or fabric store, as well as countless Internet sources.

For hand sewing, we love the ThimblePad®, a little round, stick-on, leather thimble. Using a ThimblePad, you can sew for hours without soreness in your pushing finger. You can stick one on your sewing machine or scissors so it will always be handy.

If you're an instant gratification kind of quilter, you need to know about the Angler™ by Pam Bono Designs, which lets you skip a step in making half-square and quarter-square triangles from squares. With the Angler taped to your sewing machine bed, you don't have to draw a diagonal line on your squares. Just line up the squares with the lines on the Angler and start sewing.

For machine quilting, we recommend that you invest in a walking foot or even-feed foot made for your particular sewing machine. These feet feed the layers of fabric through the machine at the same speed, helping to prevent puckers while you're quilting.

We simply couldn't work without the Appliqué Pressing Sheet™ by Bear Thread Designs. Our only complaint is that it isn't big enough to cover a full-size ironing board!

For hours of fun designing your own quilts, trying out different fabrics and color schemes, and even sharing "virtual" projects with online friends, you can't beat EQ5 by the Electric Quilt Company.

must-know techniques

SIZE *DOES* MATTER

In quilting, at least. That's because seam size is smaller in quilting patterns than it is in patterns for clothing and other crafts. Unless the pattern specifies a different size, virtually all quilting patterns expect you to use a 1/4"-wide seam allowance. Before you start sewing, test your machine to find out how you can achieve an accurate, consistent 1/4" seam. You may be able to purchase a 1/4" foot for your machine. If you can't, then you have a couple of options: you can move the needle or move the fabric. Here's how to find the 1/4" point on your machine.

First, find a piece of card stock that's approximately 3" x 5". (Those annoying tear-out advertising cards in magazines are perfect for this, as are recipe cards for dishes you're never going to make.) Second, line up the edge of the card with the 1/4" mark on your rotary ruler, and draw a fine line 1/4" from the edge of the card.

Now you're ready to set up your machine. If you can't move your needle to the left and right, do the following: With the line on the right-hand side of the card, put the card under the needle on your sewing machine and manually lower the needle until it goes right through the drawn line. Take a piece of masking tape and stick it to the bed of your sewing machine along the right edge of the card. (Fig. 1) When you sew, line up the edges of your fabric with the left edge of the masking tape.

If you can move the needle on your machine, then first attach your favorite presser foot to the machine. With the drawn line on the right-hand side of the card, put the card underneath the presser foot so it lines up with the right edge of the foot. Now slowly lower your needle by hand until it's slightly above the card. Move the needle to the right or left, as needed, until the needle will come down right through the drawn line. (Fig. 2) Make a note of this needle position, and always set the needle at the same position when you sew seams for your quilts. Then you can line up your fabric with the right side of the presser foot and get an accurate 1/4" seam.

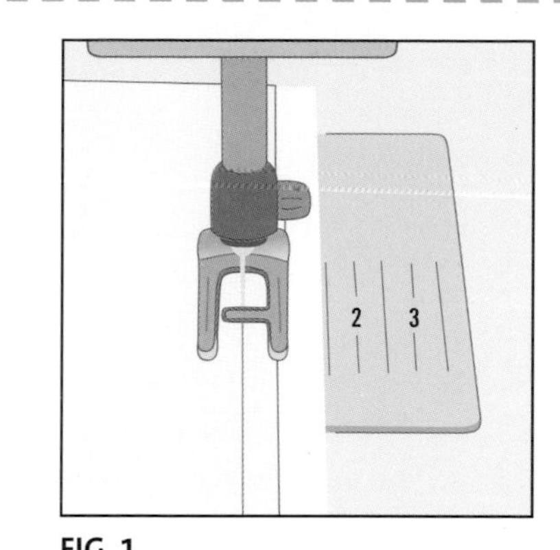

FIG. 1

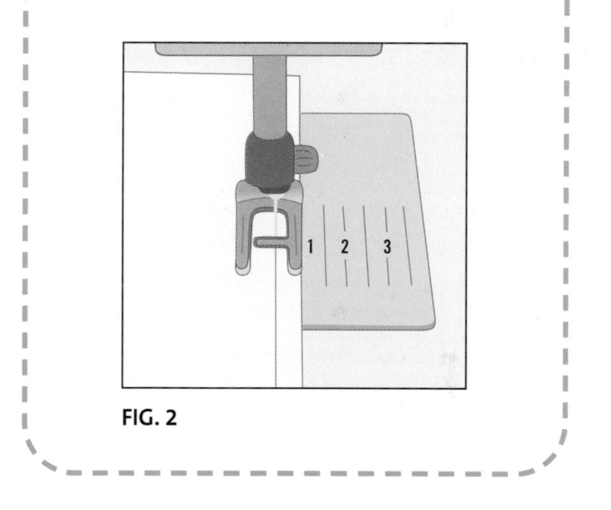

FIG. 2

Test it out. Even with a 1/4" presser foot, different people often sew different seam widths. Therefore, when you've finished setting up your machine to sew 1/4" seams, do a quick test to see if you're actually sewing a 1/4" seam. Cut three strips of fabric 1 1/2" x 5". Sew the strips together along the 5" sides. Press seams to one side. If your 1/4" seam allowance is accurate, the center strip should be 1" wide. If it isn't, adjust your seam allowance accordingly.

OPPOSITES ATTRACT

Some blocks have several pieces that are sewn together in rows (for example, the nine-patch block in Fig. 3). Pressing the seams in opposite directions on alternating rows will allow the seams to butt up against each other and line up accurately. (Fig. 4) In quilting, unless the pattern tells you otherwise, *always press seams to one side*, rather than pressing them open. As a general rule, press toward the darker fabric.

JOIN THE CHAIN GANG

When you're making the same block or unit several times, you can set up the pieces in stacks to the left of your sewing machine, and chain piece the units, one after the other, without cutting the thread and starting over after each unit. For example, let's look at a four-patch unit made up of two light squares and two dark squares. The block is made by sewing one light-dark unit, one dark-light unit, and then sewing the two units together. (Fig. 5) But these two-square units are actually the same—it's just that half of them are turned with the light fabric on the left and the other half are turned with the light fabric on the right. So they can be sewn in exactly the same way.

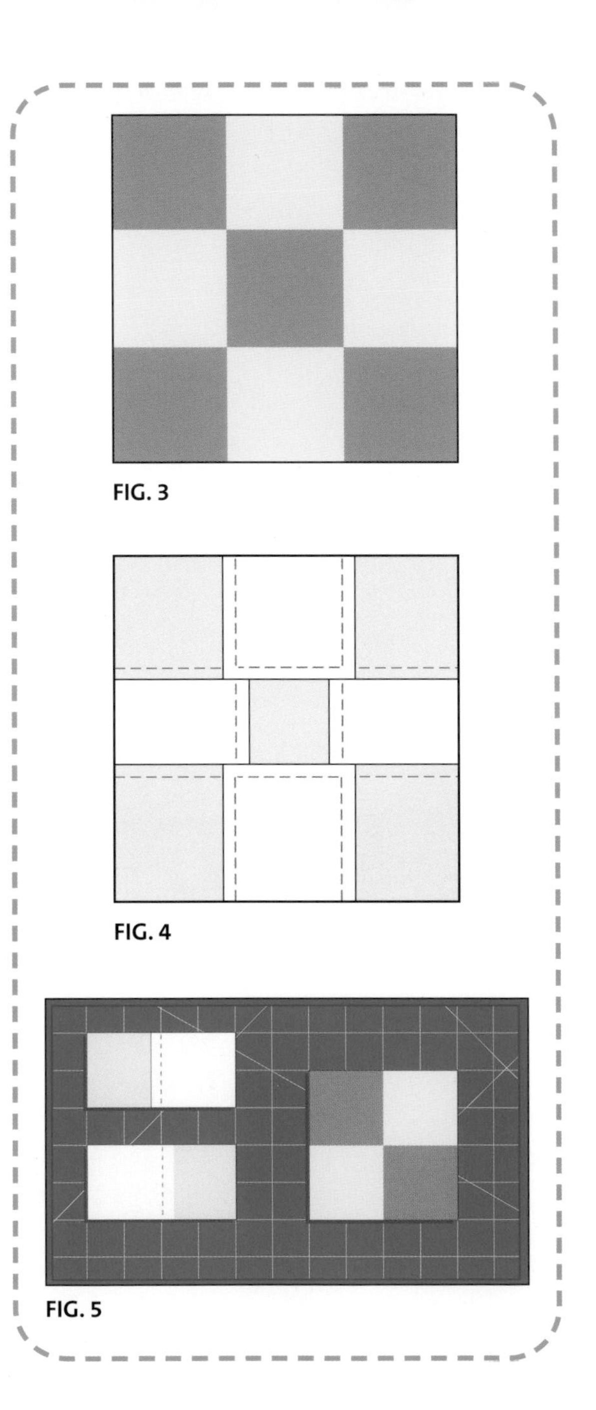

FIG. 3

FIG. 4

FIG. 5

To chain piece these units, set two piles of squares, one from each fabric, to the left of the sewing machine. Pick up one square from each fabric, place them right sides together, and sew. *Don't cut the thread.* Keep stitching a few stitches past the end of the seam. The machine stitches will create a little chain between the first unit and the next one. Pick up two more squares, place them right sides together, and lay them directly in front of the presser foot. Begin sewing again, and the machine will pull the fabric under the foot and sew the second unit.

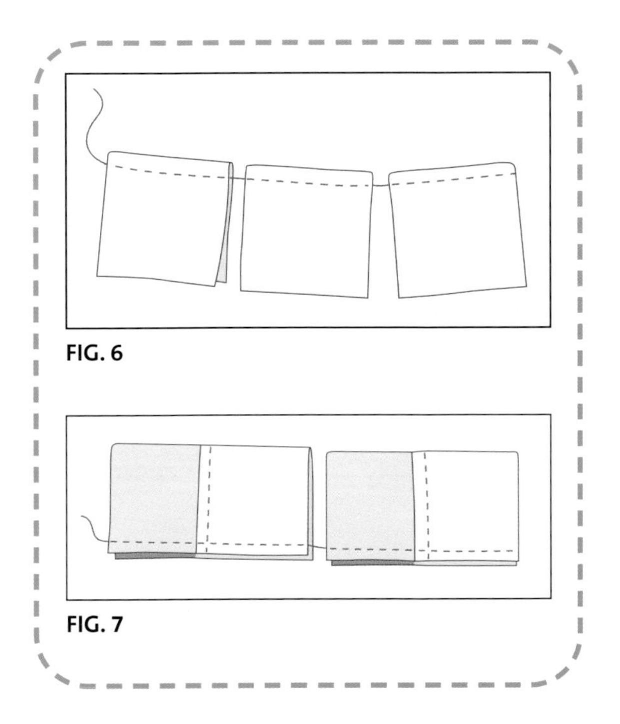

FIG. 6

FIG. 7

(Fig. 6) Using this method, you can sew together units for multiple blocks without ever stopping to cut the threads.

Next, press all the seams to one side, *in the same direction* (that is, toward the same fabric). Remember that one unit will be rotated before the units are joined, so if you press all of the seams the same way, half of them will end up going in the opposite direction and they will butt up against each other for an accurate, flat seam when they are joined. Next, make two stacks of the two-square units next to your machine. In one stack, have the light fabric on the left, and in the other stack, have the light fabric on the right. Pick up one unit from each stack, and place them right sides together, with the seams butted up against each other.

do it right: You will always know the fabrics are turned the right way if the seams are going in opposite directions and butt up against each other. If the seams are going the same way, one of the units must be turned around.

Now sew the units together, but again, *don't cut the threads*. Just as you did with the smaller units, sew a few stitches past the end of the seam and feed the next set of units through in the same way. (Fig. 7) In a very short time, you can complete dozens of four-patch blocks.

This method works not just for four-patches, or even just for units made from squares. You can use the same method whenever you have to do the same step over and over to make several units, whether you're sewing squares, rectangles, triangles, or other shapes.

You can also chain piece units that have been cut from strip-pieced fabrics; for example, to make the first set of units for four-patch

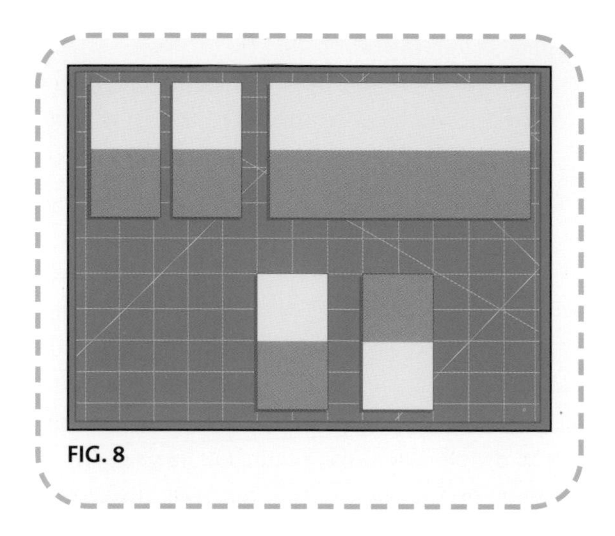
FIG. 8

blocks, instead of cutting individual squares and sewing them together, cut strips instead. Sew together one light strip and one dark strip, and press the seam to one side. Then cut the strip unit into segments the same width as your original strips; for example, if your strips were 2 1/2" wide, cut your segments 2 1/2" wide. (Fig. 8) Next make stacks of the units as described above, and chain piece them together to complete the four-patch blocks.

TRIANGLES ARE SQUARE?

Some of the patterns in this book require half-square triangles. When the pattern allows it, it's much easier to make half-square triangles from squares of fabric than it is to cut triangles and then stitch them together. Cut triangles have a long, bias edge that tends to stretch and distort. Making half-square triangles from squares keeps them more accurate.

Cut squares of fabric in the size listed in the pattern. On the wrong side of the lighter squares, draw a diagonal line from corner to corner. (Fig. 9) Place each lighter-colored square on a darker square, right sides together. Next, stitch a scant 1/4" on *each* side of the drawn line. (Fig. 10) Finally, cut *on* the drawn line, and press the seam to one side. Each set of squares will yield two half-square triangle units. (Fig. 11)

Square up the half-square triangles to the required size. When squaring, be sure the diagonal seam continues to run from corner to corner. Small, square rotary rulers make this step a breeze.

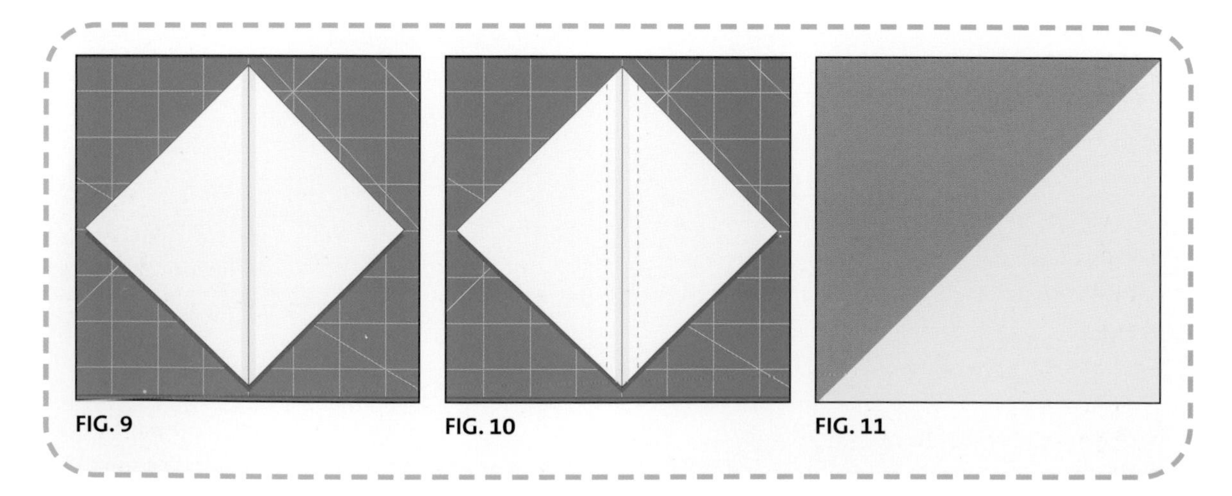
FIG. 9 FIG. 10 FIG. 11

APPLIQUÉ THE EASY WAY

- The appliqué projects in this book can be completed by hand or machine. To make appliqué quick and easy, use a fusible webbing or fusible adhesive (such as Lite Steam-A-Seam 2®, Wonder-Under®, Heat'n Bond Lite®, or Fine Fuse® Fusible Adhesive), freezer paper, fusible interfacing, or water-soluble glue stick to adhere the appliqué pieces to the background before stitching. Fusible interfacing will produce a finished edge to the appliqué. The other methods will leave a raw edge.
- To use a **glue stick**, or other washable basting glue (we love Roxanne's Glue-Baste-It®), cut out the appliqué shapes from your fabric using templates. (See Terrific Templates, opposite.) Apply glue to the back of the appliqué shape and place the shape on the background fabric. Wait for the glue to dry before stitching.
- To use **fusible webbing**, or **fusible adhesive**, buy the most lightweight fusible you can find, to leave the finished piece soft and supple. Trace the appliqué pattern onto one side of the fusible. Note: Check to see if the appliqué pattern has been reversed for tracing. If not, you must reverse the pattern. Cut out the shape 1/4" to 1/2" *outside* the drawn line, and fuse to the wrong side of your appliqué fabric following the manufacturer's directions. Next, cut out the shape *on* the drawn line. Fuse the appliqué piece in place on the background fabric, and secure the edges of the appliqué shape using hand or machine stitching.
- To use **fusible interfacing**, trace the appliqué pattern onto the nonfusible side of the interfacing. Note: In this method, the appliqué pattern should *not* be reversed. Cut out the shape 1/4" to 1/2" *outside* the drawn line. Place (but don't fuse) the fusible side of the interfacing against the right side of the appliqué fabric. Stitch *on* the drawn line, and then trim 1/8" to 1/4" outside the stitching. Carefully cut a slit in the center of the interfacing, and turn inside out. The right side of the appliqué fabric and the fusible side of the interfacing will be on the outside. Finger press around the edge of the appliqué. Fuse the appliqué in place on the background fabric following the interfacing manufacturer's instructions. Secure the edges of the appliqué using hand or machine stitching.
- **Terrific Templates.** Some of the projects in this book require you to make templates for the appliqué shapes. Although you can make

permanent templates from template plastic or other permanent materials, there are less expensive alternatives. You can trace appliqué shapes directly onto the back of fusibles and fabrics using a light box, or by taping the pattern and fabric to a sunny window. You can cut the appliqué shapes from freezer paper (available at the grocery store), which has a waxy back. With the waxy side down, iron the shape onto your fabric, draw or cut around it, and then easily peel it off. You can even cut the shape out of paper scraps you have around the house (grocery sacks, magazine tear-out cards, and so on), pin or glue-stick the shapes to your fabric, and trace or cut around the shapes. The bottom line: don't stress yourself out if you don't have the materials for the exact method listed in a pattern. Use what you have on hand; it'll work out fine!

- **Enlarging Images.** Many of the appliqué patterns instruct you to enlarge the pattern by a specified percentage. You can take the pattern to your local copy shop and have it enlarged.

  If you have access to an overhead projector, another option is to tape poster paper to a wall, project the pattern in the appropriate size onto the poster paper, and trace the outline, right on the poster paper.

READY, SET, QUILT!

Once you finish the quilt top, get ready to quilt. Make a **backing** (also called the lining) that's at least 5" wider and 5" longer than the quilt top. If your backing has to be more than 40" wide, you will have to piece it. To use a single fabric, add a strip of fabric to each side of the center. (Fig. 12) If you simply sew two lengths of fabric together, the seam will be in the middle. Quilts often are folded in the middle, creating more stress on a center seam. Therefore, it's better to have the seams off center.

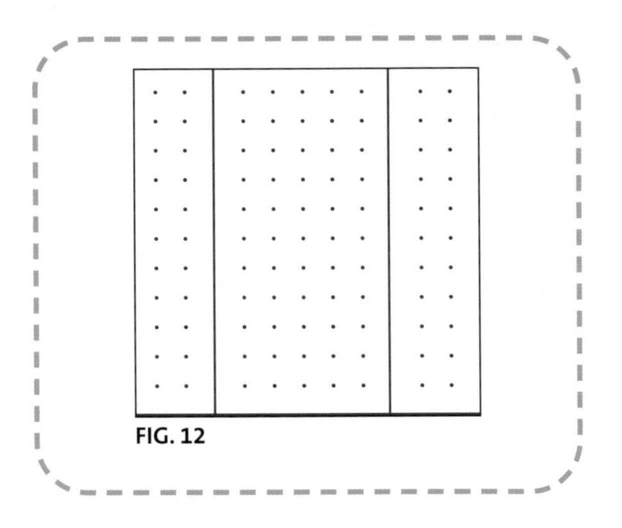
FIG. 12

Rather than using just a single fabric, you can have some fun using leftover scraps and block units to piece a backing that coordinates with the quilt top. See the back of Makin' Me Dizzy as an example.

After the backing is made, make a quilt sandwich by layering the backing (wrong side up), the batting, and the quilt top (right side up). **Baste** all the layers together to prevent puckers while quilting. If you will be hand quilting, use white thread and baste the layers by hand in a 3" to 4" grid. (No matter how long the basting stays on the quilt, white thread won't bleed.) If you will be machine quilting, you may choose to baste using safety pins. Be sure to use sharp, stainless steel safety pins to prevent rust stains on your quilt. A third choice is to use a basting spray or fusible batting to

hold the layers together during quilting.

When the layers are basted together, quilt as desired, by hand or machine. Several common quilting patterns are **quilting in the ditch**, which means outlining patches by quilting on or very near the seam lines; **echo quilting**, which involves following the outline of a shape, then repeating the outline again and again at a fixed distance (such as $\frac{1}{2}$") until you reach the edge of the area (see, for example, the quilting on Indigo Nights); **stippling**, which is a method of free-motion quilting that fills in background areas with a continuous curly line of quilting; and **meandering**, which is like stippling, but larger and with the quilting lines farther apart, often used to cover the entire face of an informal quilt.

finishing with flair

You may not actually find a pot of gold at the end of the rainbow, but finishing a quilt provides its own special kind of satisfaction. These final steps will lead you to the end of your rainbow, as you complete your quilted projects with a flair.

FIRST-RATE BINDINGS

Some quilters hate binding, often because they have trouble getting their bindings to lie flat, have square corners, and look sharp and neat. The problem? It's all in the pressing. To achieve beautiful bindings, you must press the binding *four* separate times.

For a basic narrow binding, start by cutting $2\frac{1}{8}$" strips. For quilts with straight edges, cut strips from the lengthwise grain of the fabric (parallel to the selvage edge), rather than crosswise (perpendicular to the selvages), when possible. For quilts with curved edges, cut strips on the bias. Sew strips together using a diagonal seam and a short stitch length (2.0 mm) until you have a piece of binding long enough to go all the way around your quilt, plus 12" to 15".

- **Pressing #1:** Press the strips in half lengthwise, wrong sides together, using steam. (Fig. 13)

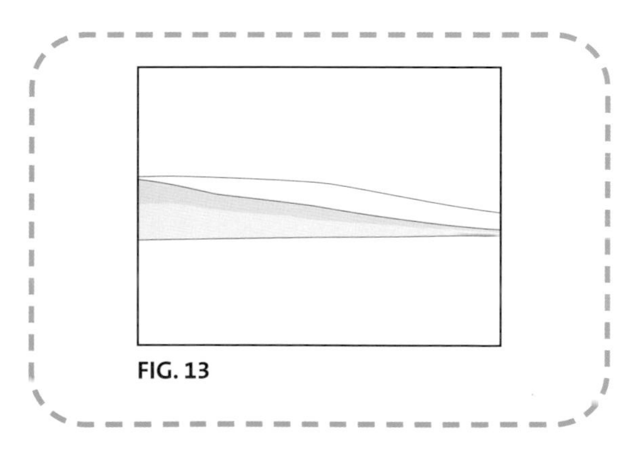

FIG. 13

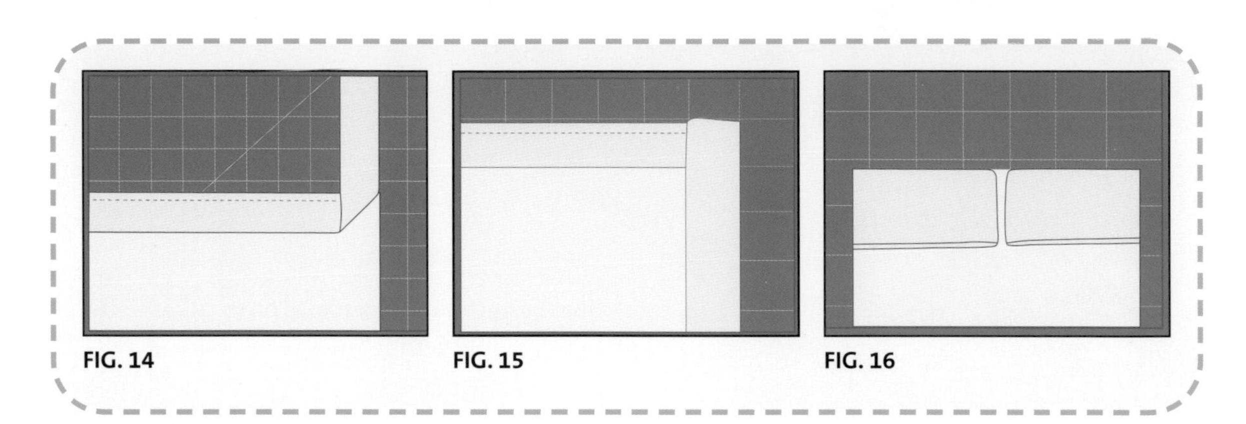
FIG. 14 FIG. 15 FIG. 16

Beginning in the middle of one side of the quilt, join the binding to the quilt using a 1/4" seam and a short stitch length (2.0 mm). Leave a loose tail 6" long at the beginning before you begin sewing. As you sew, hold the binding taut, but *don't stretch it*. Stop sewing 1/4" before you reach the corner. Cut the threads and remove the quilt from underneath the needle. Turn the quilt with the next side to be sewn on the right. Flip up the binding so it's even with the side of the quilt and it makes a 45° triangle at the corner. (Fig. 14) Then fold it back down even with the quilt's edge. (Fig. 15)

Begin stitching about 1/8" from the corner and stitch *back* to the corner; then stitch forward, attaching the binding to the quilt and stopping 1/4" before the next corner. Continue in the same way until you're almost back to the starting point. Stop sewing 8" to 10" from where you started.

Bring the two ends of the binding together in the center of the remaining open space and fold them back, *leaving a small space* (about 1/4") in between the two pieces. (Fig. 16) Crease the folds with your fingernail. Open up the binding and use a light pencil line to mark the lengthwise and crosswise folds.

Place the two ends right sides together at a right angle to each other. Align the pieces along the drawn lines, and pin. (Fig. 17) Stitch a diagonal seam to join the ends. *Before trimming the seam*, fold and position the binding to be sure it fits well, and also to be sure you are trimming on the correct side of the seam. Then press the seam *open* before you trim. Trim each side of the seam, press to restore the fold in the binding, and then finish stitching the binding to the quilt.

- **Pressing #2:** Press the binding flat, just as you have sewn it, using steam.

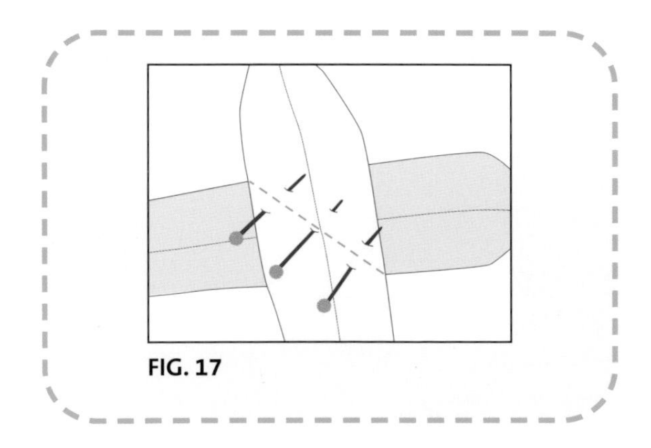
FIG. 17

- **Pressing #3:** Press the binding up, away from the quilt, using steam. (Fig. 18)
- **Pressing #4:** Turn the quilt over. Pull the binding up and over the quilt's edge, and back down toward you, covering the stitching that attached the binding to the front. Press the binding using a hot iron. As you come to each corner, fold and press a miter. (Fig. 19) Use steam at your own risk: it helps flatten the binding, but it's very easy to burn your fingers!

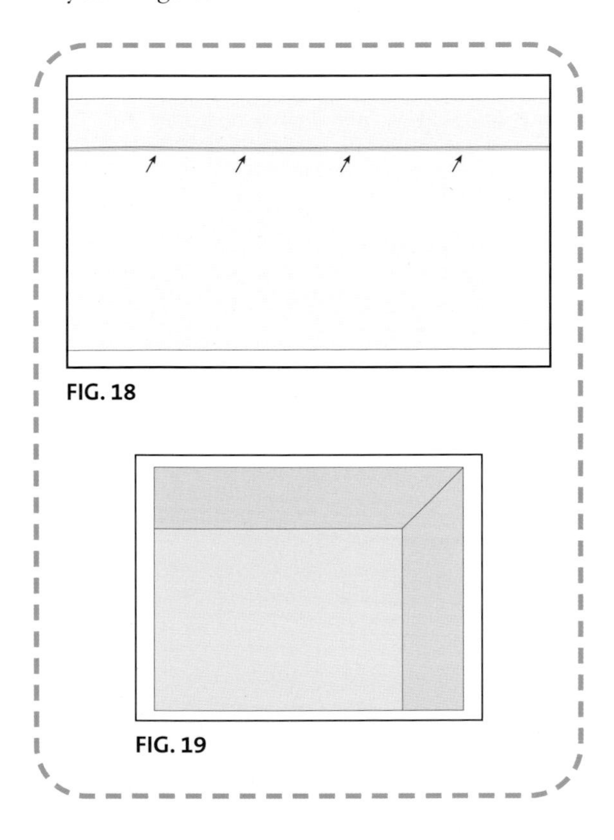

FIG. 18

FIG. 19

Stitch the binding to the quilt. If the second side of your binding will be hand stitched to the quilt, machine stitch the binding to the *front* of the quilt, and then hand stitch the second side to the back. If the second side of your binding will be machine stitched to the quilt, stitch the binding to the *back* of the quilt first, and then machine stitch the binding to the front of the quilt. When you're finished, close the miters at each corner by hand with a few tiny stitches.

If you press the binding all four times as above, you will be able to stitch the second side of your binding to the quilt without having to use pins to hold the binding in place as you stitch. Your finished binding will be full, flat, and have nice, sharp corners.

BE A SHOW-OFF

Whether you make a full-size Quirky Quilt or a smaller project, you'll enjoy sharing your triumph with friends and family. You may even want to enter a quilt show. Using the following instructions, you can add a hanging sleeve to your quilt that will accommodate a dowel or rod without curling the top of your quilt to the back.

Most quilt shows require a 4" sleeve, so these instructions are for a 4" sleeve. For a smaller wall hanging or miniature quilt, decrease the measurements for the size dowel or rod you plan to use to hang the quilt.

1. Cut (or piece, if necessary) a length of fabric that is 9" wide and as long as the width of your quilt. For example, if your quilt is 72" x 90", the sleeve fabric should be 9" x 72".
2. Fold the fabric in half (so it's now 4½" wide), *wrong* sides together, and sew down the long edge using a ½" seam.
3. Position the seam in the center of the tube (rather than at the top or bottom edge), and press the seam to one side. (The seam allowance is on the *outside* of the tube.)
4. Finish the ends of the tube using a narrow hem, as follows. Fold the raw edge on one end to the inside of the tube ¼" and press. Then fold in another ¼", hiding the raw edge, and press again. Stitch by hand or machine, close to the inner folded edge. Repeat for the other end of the tube. Press after stitching. You now have a tube with finished ends that is 4" wide and 1" shorter than the width of your quilt.

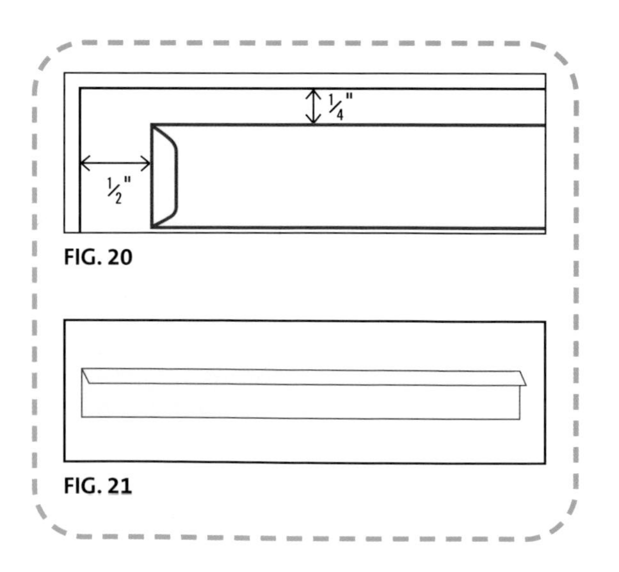

FIG. 20

FIG. 21

5. Find the center of the sleeve length and insert a pin. Find the center of the top edge of your quilt and insert a pin.
6. Matching the centers, lay the sleeve on the back of the quilt with the seam allowance against the quilt (on the underside of the sleeve), and the top edge of the sleeve about ¼" below the top of the quilt. The sleeve ends should be ½" from the outer sides of the quilt. Pin the sleeve in place. (Fig. 20)
7. Appliqué the bottom edge of the sleeve to the quilt.
8. Fold the top edge of the sleeve down 1" and press. (Fig. 21) Pin this newly pressed edge in place, taking care to pin only the bottom layer of the sleeve to the quilt: you will only be stitching the bottom layer of the sleeve to the quilt. Appliqué the newly pressed edge to the quilt. Appliqué the ends of the sleeve from the newly pressed edge down to the bottom of the sleeve.
9. After you have finished stitching the sleeve to the quilt, press the 1" you folded down back up (in other words, press the sleeve flat again). When you insert the dowel or rod into the sleeve, the unattached 1" at the top will allow your quilt to hang straight and flat.
10. As an alternative to a sleeve, you can sew fabric tabs to the quilt's top and allow the hanging rod to show. For very small quilts, you can sew plastic rings on the upper back corners, or even use tabs from soft drink cans as inexpensive, quick hangers.

MAKE IT PERSONAL

A quilt isn't really finished until you add a label. You may choose simply to add your signature and a date, or you may want to use fabric paints or your ink-jet printer and treated fabric to create something really special. A label might include your name, the date of completion, the name of the quilt, and something about the person receiving the quilt or the occasion for which the quilt was made. You can make the label early enough to piece it into the quilt's back, or you can appliqué the label to the back after you finish the binding. Usually labels are located on the lower left-hand corner of the quilt back, but anything goes—sometimes labels even appear on the front.

And now it's time to quilt!

difficulty ratings

These icons appear next to every project to indicate their challenge quotient. Think about your skill level and how much time you want to spend, then go from there.

= **Very Easy.** These projects have simple instructions, require little or no prior quilting experience, and can be completed in a few hours. Great for quick gifts or a fun afternoon.

= **Easy.** These projects also have simple instructions, but they'll take longer to make. Most can be finished in a weekend (except for the actual quilting of the larger projects). Some sewing or quilting experience will be helpful, but it isn't required if you take your time and read the instructions thoroughly.

= **Moderate.** These projects take longer to complete (like the Shoo-Fly Rag Throw), require more intricate piecing (like the Makin' Me Dizzy Quilt), or present more challenging techniques (like the Hearts Afire Quilt or the Mum's the Word Wall Hanging). Some quilting experience is required to finish these projects successfully. (Or enlist the help of a friend who's an experienced quilter—always a nice thing to have!)

= **Difficult.** You'll be very happy to learn that there are no difficult projects in this book!

METRIC CONVERSION CHART

fractions of one inch

3/16"	0.5cm
5/8"	1.5cm
3/8"	1cm
1/8"	0.3cm
1/4"	0.6cm
1/2"	1.3cm
2/3"	1.8cm
3/4"	1.9cm

whole inch measurements

1"	2.5cm
2"	5cm
3"	7.5cm
4"	10cm
5"	12.5cm
6"	15cm
7"	17.5cm
8"	20cm
9"	22.5cm
10"	25cm
12"	30cm
13"	32.5cm
14"	35cm
15"	37.5cm
16"	40cm
17"	42.5cm
18"	45cm
19"	47.5cm
20"	50cm
22"	55cm
23"	57.5cm
24"	60cm
25"	62.5cm
26"	65cm
29"	72.5cm
30"	75cm
31"	77.5cm
34"	85cm
36"	90cm
37"	92.5cm
38"	95cm
40"	100cm
42"	105cm
43"	107.5cm
44"	110cm
45"	112.5cm
46"	115cm
48"	120cm
49"	122.5cm
50"	125cm
51"	127.5cm
54"	135cm
56"	140cm
58"	145cm
60"	150cm
63"	157.5cm
65"	162.5cm
66"	165cm
68"	170cm
70"	175cm
72"	180cm
74"	185cm
77"	192.5cm
86"	215cm
90"	225cm
91"	227.5cm
93"	232.5cm
103"	257.5cm
107"	267.5cm

inch-plus measurements

1 1/2"	3.8cm
1 3/4"	4.4cm
2 1/8"	5.3cm
2 1/2"	6.3cm
3 1/4"	8.1cm
3 1/2"	8.8cm
4 1/4"	10.6cm
4 1/2"	11.3cm
5 1/4"	13.1cm
5 3/8"	13.5cm
5 1/2"	13.8cm
6 1/8"	15.3cm
6 1/4"	15.6cm
6 1/2"	16.3cm
6 3/4"	16.9cm
7 3/8"	18.5cm
7 1/2"	18.8cm
8 1/2"	21.3cm
8 3/4"	21.9cm
9 1/4"	23.1cm
10 1/2"	26.3cm
11 3/4"	29.4cm
12 1/4"	30.6cm
12 1/2"	31.3cm
13 3/4"	34.4cm
14 1/4"	35.6cm
14 1/2"	36.3cm
15 1/2"	38.8cm
15 3/4"	39.4cm
16 1/2"	41.3cm
16 3/4"	41.9cm
17 1/2"	43.8cm
18 1/2"	46.3cm
19 1/2"	48.8cm
21 3/4"	54.4cm
22 3/4"	56.9cm
28 1/2"	71.3cm
29 1/2"	73.8cm
30 1/2"	76.3cm
31 1/2"	78.8cm
33 1/2"	83.8cm
36 1/2"	91.3cm
46 1/2"	116.3cm
47 1/2"	118.8cm
50 1/2"	125.6cm

yardage

1/8 yd	11.3cm
1/4 yd	0.2m
1/3 yd	30cm
1/2 yd	0.5m
2/3 yd	60cm
3/4 yd	0.7m
1 yd	0.9m
1 1/4 yd	1.1m
1 1/3 yd	120cm
1 1/2 yd	1.3m
1 2/3 yd	150cm
2 yd	1.8m
2 1/3 yd	210cm
2 2/3 yd	240cm
3 yd	2.7m
3 3/4 yd	3.4m
5 yd	4.5m
5 1/4 yd	4.7m
6 1/2 yd	5.9m

if you've got it, flaunt it!

From a small eye-popping quilt to a fake fur pillow, the patterns in this chapter have personality—and encourage you to express yours too. Throw the Makin' Me Dizzy Quilt over the back of a chair or across a coffee table, or liven up a room when you hang it on your wall. Make and send the Let's Celebrate! Fabric Card in recognition of a special someone's special occasion, whether it's a birthday, graduation, or job promotion. Unleash the animal in you with the quick and easy Jungle Fever Pillow made in one of the many realistic fake furs on the market today, or substitute a soft suede or slinky velvet that strikes your fancy. Take a nap by the fire, curl up with a good book, or watch your favorite show, relaxing to your heart's content with the ultrasoft Hearts Afire Quilt.

makin' me dizzy quilt

MAKIN' ME DIZZY MADE BY TOMME J. FENT
QUILTED BY JAN GIBSON-KORYTKOWSKI

Irregular stripes, polka dots, and bright colors combine in a dizzying op art design in this lap-size quilt that can also be used as a wall hanging. Strip piecing and clever cutting using triangle rulers make the blocks and borders fast and fun! Use leftover fabric from the quilt top to add unexpected interest to the back of your quilt.

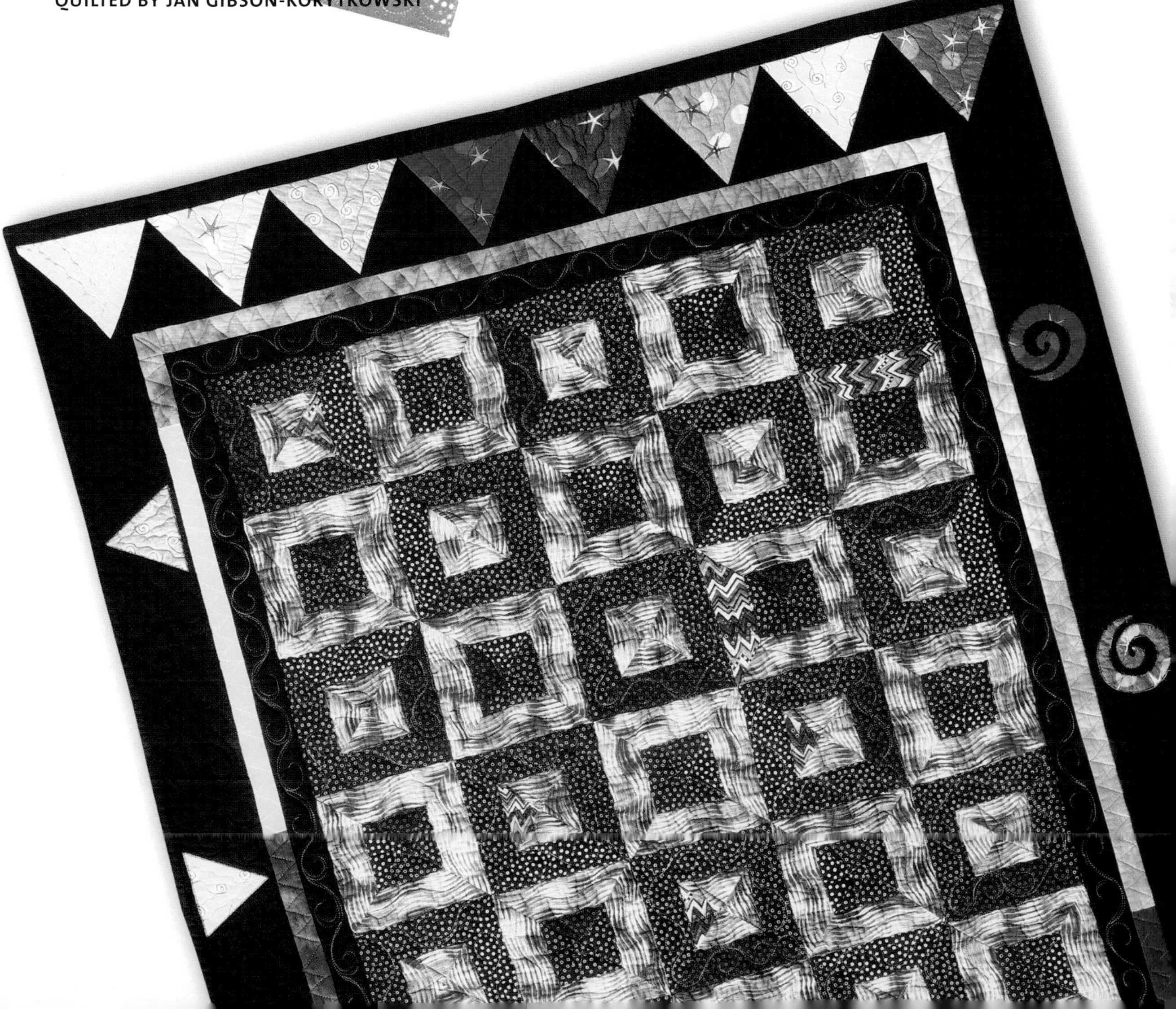

DESIGNER

Tomme J. Fent

FINISHED SIZE

43" x 58"

FINISHED BLOCK SIZE

6" square

MATERIALS

Fabric A: 1 1/4 yd. bright-colored striped fabric

Fabric B: 1 1/4 yd. (total) contrasting fabrics (photo quilt uses black with dots in red, blue, green, yellow, purple, and pink)

Fabric C: 1/8 yd. each of 8 bright prints (1 yd. total) for pieced triangles in top and bottom borders, and appliquéd triangles and spirals in side borders

Fabric D: 1/8 yd. each (3/4 yd. total) of several bright solids for inner border (photo quilt uses red, orange, green, blue, purple, and yellow)

Fabric E: 1 1/2 yd. solid black, for borders and binding

Backing: 2 2/3 yd. backing fabric(s)

Fusible webbing: enough for six 3 1/2" squares

45° triangle ruler

60° triangle ruler

CUTTING

Fabric A: Cut 36 strips 2" x 20" along the length of the stripe (for blocks). (In other words, if the stripe runs the width of the fabric, from selvage to selvage, then cut strips across the width of the fabric. If the stripe runs lengthwise, parallel to the selvage edge, then cut strips lengthwise.)

Fabric B: Cut 36 strips (total) from the assorted fabrics, 2" x 20" (for blocks).

Fabric C: From each print, cut two 6 1/8" squares (for pieced triangle border, top and bottom).

- From 6 of the prints, cut one 3 1/2" square (for appliqués in outer side borders).

Fabric D: From each color, cut strips 1 1/2" wide. Join strips at short ends using a straight seam to make 2 strips 48" long and 2 strips 38" long (for inner border).

Fabric E: Cut the following border strips from lengthwise grain of fabric. Measurements are slightly longer than required.

- 2 strips 2" x 36" (inner border, top and bottom)
- 2 strips 2" x 46" (inner border, sides)
- 2 strips 4 1/2" x 48" (outer border, sides)
- 2 strips 6 1/8" x 24" (pieced triangle border, top and bottom) (Cut 1 strip 6 1/8" x length of fabric, and then cut 24" lengths from this strip.)
- 2 strips 2" x 50" (outer border, top and bottom)
- 4 strips 2 1/8" x length of fabric (for binding)

CONSTRUCTION

MAKING THE BLOCKS, USING THE 45° TRIANGLE RULER

1. Join a Fabric A strip to a Fabric B strip along the long sides of the strips. Press seam away from Fabric A and toward Fabric B. Repeat until all Fabric A strips are joined to Fabric B strips. You will end up with 36 strips that are now 3 1/2" x 20".
2. Lay the 45° triangle ruler, with the right angle at the top, on the strip. Line up the 2" line with the seam line between Fabric A and Fabric B. (Fig. 1) Cut along both sides of the ruler.

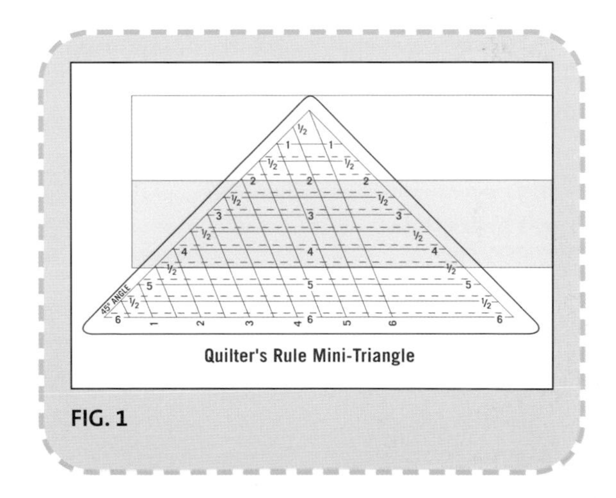

FIG. 1

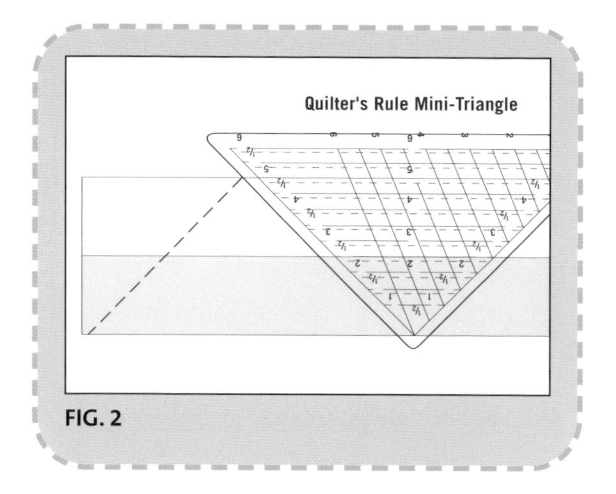

FIG. 2

3. Turn the ruler 180° so the right angle is at the bottom and the side is lined up with the cut edge from the first triangle. (Fig. 2) Cut along the opposite side.
4. Repeat steps 2 and 3 with each 20" strip for a total of 144 triangles. (You'll actually only need 140 triangles: 68 of one kind and 72 of the other.)
5. Select two triangles that have Fabric A on the long side and Fabric B on the short side. Place the triangles right sides together, aligning the seam lines. Stitch using a 1/4" seam allowance. (Fig. 3) Press seam to one side.

do it right: When making units from two triangles, always press the seams in the same direction; for example, with the long, flat side facing you, always press the seam to the right. Then when you join the units to make the block, your seams will be opposing, reducing bulk. See Opposites Attract on page 10.

6. Repeat step 5 with two more triangles that have Fabric A on the long side and Fabric B on the short side. Press seam to one side.
7. Join the units from steps 5 and 6 to finish the block. (Fig. 4)
8. Repeat steps 5, 6, and 7 to make a total of **17 blocks** that have Fabric A on the outside and Fabric B on the inside.
9. Repeat steps 5, 6, and 7 with the remaining triangles (this time with Fabric B on the long side and Fabric A on the short side), to make a total of **18 blocks** that have Fabric B on the outside and Fabric A on the inside. (Fig. 5)

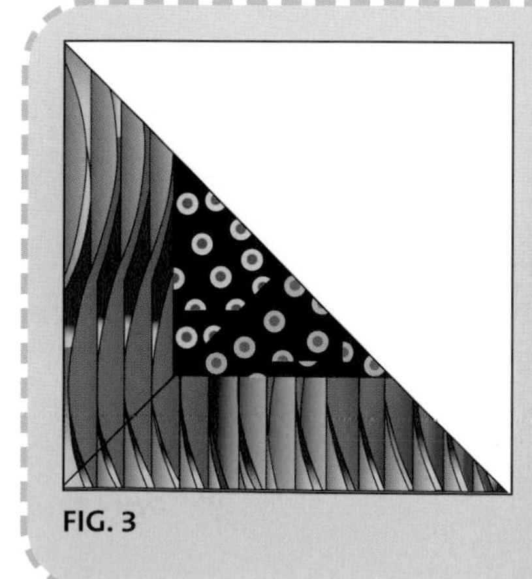

FIG. 3

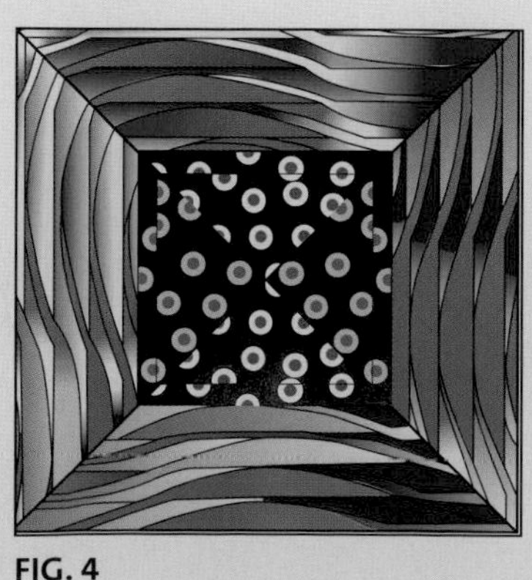

FIG. 4

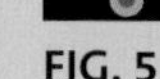

FIG. 5

FIG. 6

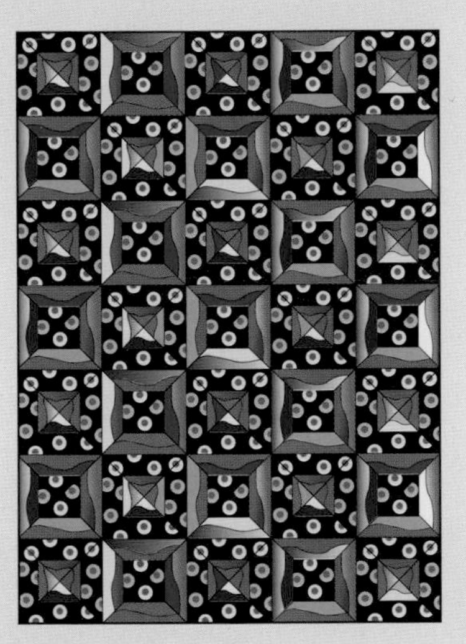

FIG. 7

FIG. 8

10. Join the blocks into 7 rows of 5 blocks each, alternating the two types of blocks. (Fig. 6) Begin Rows 2, 4, and 6 with a block having Fabric A on the outside, and press seams to the left. Begin Rows 1, 3, 5, and 7 with a block having Fabric B on the outside, and press seams to the right.

11. Join rows, matching seams between blocks. (Fig. 7)

ADDING THE INNER BORDERS

1. Measure the length of the quilt (top to bottom) through the center. (Fig. 8)

do it right: To avoid wavy borders, always measure through the center of the quilt. The sides tend to stretch a bit as you sew.

2. Cut the 2" x 46" Fabric E strips to match the length measurement. Stitch one strip to each long side of the quilt.

3. Measure the width of the quilt (side to side) through the center. (Fig. 8) Cut the 2" x 36" Fabric E strips to match the width measurement. Stitch strips to the top and bottom of the quilt.

4. Measure the length of the quilt through the center, and cut the 1 1/2" x 48" Fabric D strips to match the length measurement. Stitch one strip to each long side of the quilt. See the photo on page 28 for placement.

5. Measure the width of the quilt through the center, and cut the 1 1/2" x 38" strips to match the width measurement. Stitch strips to the top and bottom of the quilt. Refer to the photo on page 28 for placement.

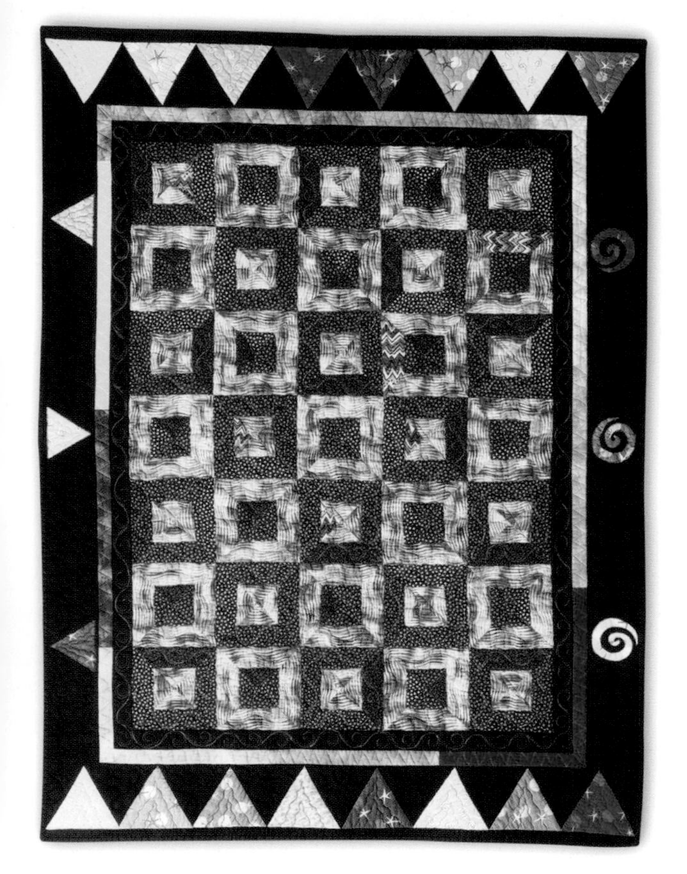

MAKING THE SIDE BORDERS

1. Measure the length of the quilt through the center, and cut the $4\frac{1}{2}$" x 48" Fabric E strips to match the length measurement. Stitch one strip to each long side of the quilt.
2. Draw free-form spirals, triangles, or other desired shapes onto the paper side of fusible webbing. Fuse webbing to the back of each $3\frac{1}{2}$" Fabric C square. Cut out shapes on drawn line. Remove paper backing and fuse shapes to the Fabric E borders on the sides of the quilt.
3. Stitch around outside of appliquéd shapes using black thread and tiny machine zigzag stitch (1.5-mm long x 2-mm wide).

MAKING THE TOP AND BOTTOM BORDERS USING THE 60° TRIANGLE RULER

1. From each of the $6\frac{1}{8}$" Fabric C squares, cut one triangle, placing the $5\frac{1}{4}$" line of the 60° triangle ruler along the bottom of the square. (Fig. 9) You will end up with two triangles from each of the eight Fabric C fabrics.
2. From each of the $6\frac{1}{8}$" x 24" Fabric E strips, cut eight 60° triangles, placing the $5\frac{1}{4}$" line of the 60° triangle ruler along one edge of the strip (see Fig. 9), then on the other edge, and alternating. Refer to Figs. 1 and 2, showing the same cutting method for the 45° triangles. You should have a total of 16 Fabric E triangles.

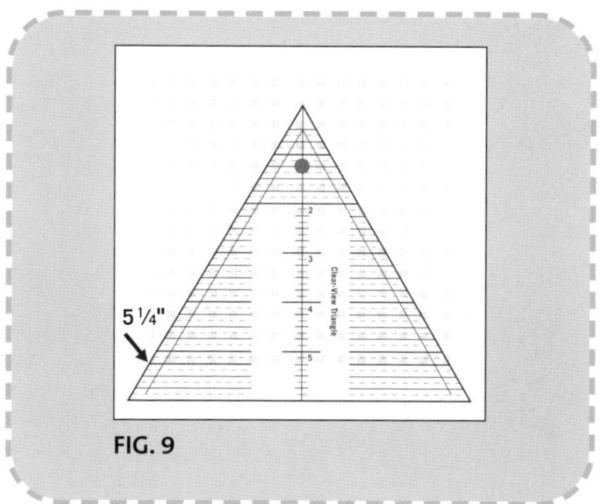

FIG. 9

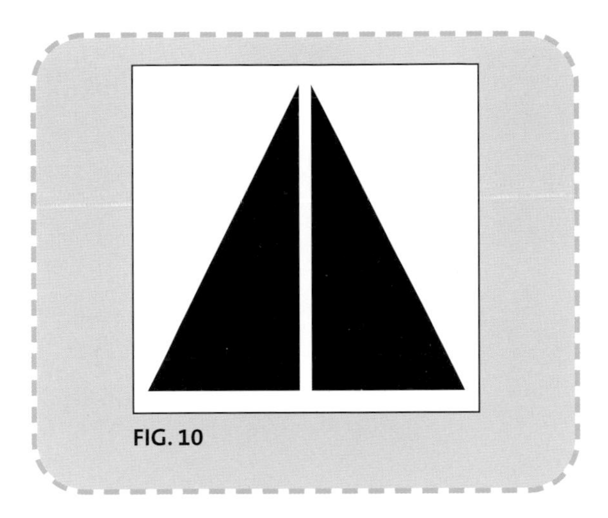
FIG. 10

3. Fold two of the Fabric E triangles in half and press very lightly. Cut the two triangles in half on the pressed line. (Fig. 10)
4. Sew triangles together into two rows, alternating Fabric C and Fabric E triangles. Each row will begin and end with one of the half-triangles from step 3. There will be eight Fabric C triangles in each row. Refer to the photo on page 28 for placement.

   do it right: Use caution when handling the 60° triangles. The bias edges will stretch easily!

5. Sew the triangle rows to the top and bottom of the quilt, with the points of the Fabric C triangles pointing in toward the center of the quilt. (See photo on page 28.)
6. Measure the width of the quilt through the center. Cut the 2" x 50" Fabric E strips to match the width measurement. Stitch strips to the top and bottom of the quilt.

FINISHING THE QUILT

If using a single fabric for the quilt back, first remove the selvages, and then cut the 2 2/3 yd. piece of backing fabric in half across the width of the fabric, making two 1 1/3 yd. pieces. From one of the 1 1/3 yd. pieces, cut two 12" strips from the length of the fabric (parallel to the selvage edge). Sew one of these narrow pieces to each side of the uncut 1 1/3 yd. piece (where the selvages used to be). The narrow strips will form the top and bottom of the quilt back, with the two seams running horizontally.

For an unexpected surprise, you can use leftover fabrics from the quilt top to make extra blocks and triangles or to cut out appliqué shapes. Add coordinating fabrics to make backing. (See photo on page 24.)

do it right: Always make the quilt back a few inches wider and longer than the quilt top to allow for shrinkage during quilting, or to allow the quilt to be loaded onto a long-arm quilting machine.

Layer the quilt top, batting, and backing, and quilt as desired. Use 2 1/8" Fabric E strips to make binding. (See First-Rate Bindings on page 15.)

To display the quilt as a wall hanging, add a hanging sleeve or hanging tabs, as desired. (See Be a Show-off on page 17.)

let's celebrate! fabric greeting card

A greeting card is always a nice way to let someone know you care. Whether you're congratulating newlyweds, sending birthday or anniversary greetings, or acknowledging the arrival of a new baby, a card you've made yourself will be especially appreciated. Customize this fabric card for whatever occasion arises simply by changing the message. The card is easy, quick, and fun to make, so let's celebrate!

Difficulty:

DESIGNER

Tomme J. Fent

FINISHED SIZE

5½" x 7½"

MATERIALS

1 fat quarter (18" x 22") yellow print for background and backing

1 rectangle 4" x 6" bright print for martini glass

1 scrap (1½" x 3½") blue fabric for liquid in glass

1 small scrap of green fabric for olive

1 tiny scrap of red-orange fabric for pimiento in olive

Small scraps for swirls, stars, or other shapes you choose

⅛ yd. lightweight fusible webbing

1 rectangle 6" x 8" of batting

Monofilament thread

Clear glass or plastic seed beads for bubbles in glass

2 permanent gel pens or fabric markers in lively colors

1 fine-tipped black permanent marker (such as Sakura's Pigma Micron®, Black 05)

1 piece heavy cardboard or mat board, 5⅜" x 7⅜"

Glue stick or narrow, double-sided tape

CONSTRUCTION

1. Trace individual patterns for martini glass, liquid, olive, and pimiento onto separate pieces of paper backing of fusible webbing (patterns are already reversed for tracing). Fuse each pattern piece to corresponding fabric, following manufacturer's instructions, and cut out on drawn line.
2. Cut a 7" x 9" rectangle of yellow print. Fuse martini glass to rectangle, with glass centered horizontally and bottom of glass 1" from bottom of rectangle. Using pattern as a guide, fuse liquid, olive, and pimiento on top of martini glass.
3. Cut two or three 2" squares of fusible webbing, and fuse to the back of scraps. Cut free-form swirls, stars, rectangles, or whatever shapes you choose, and fuse the shapes to the background around the martini glass.
4. Using a disappearing marker or masking tape, mark a straight line on the top of the card, approx. ¾" above the top of the martini glass. Trace the Let's Celebrate! lettering (below) onto the yellow background fabric with the black fine-tipped marker, using the line to keep the lettering straight. (Or write your own greeting directly on the fabric using the black marker.) Next use the bright gel pens or fabric markers to outline the black lettering.

do it right: If you don't have a light box for tracing the lettering onto the fabric, first trace the lettering onto a white piece of paper with a dark black pen or marker. Then tape the paper to a window, and tape your fabric over the paper, lining up the straight line you marked with the bottom of the lettering.

5. Center the card over the batting and machine baste all the way around the edges.
6. Thread your sewing machine with monofilament thread in the top *and* bobbin.

7. Set your machine for a short, narrow zigzag stitch (1.5 mm long x 2.0 mm wide). Starting on the bottom of the martini glass, stitch clockwise all the way around the glass, making sure the left-hand swing of the zigzag stitch catches the glass fabric and the right-hand swing of the stitch falls on the background fabric. Then zigzag around the liquid, olive, pimiento, and fused shapes. Optional: Outline the lettering using a straight stitch.

8. Thread a hand-sewing needle with monofilament thread, and tie a good knot (or two) in the end. Hand stitch several clear seed beads randomly in the liquid area of the glass. Knot thread in the back.
9. Trim the card and batting to 6" x 8", making sure the martini glass is centered. Cut another 6" x 8" rectangle of the yellow print. Place the yellow rectangle right sides together with the card front. Machine stitch a scant 1/4" all the way around the sides and top of the card, with the batting against the feed dogs of your machine and the wrong side of the backing rectangle facing up. *Leave the entire bottom open.* Turn the card right side out and press from the back.
10. Insert the cardboard or mat board through the bottom, sliding it neatly up into the top corners. (Trim the card slightly to fit, if necessary.)
11. Apply glue or double-sided tape to the bottom of the cardboard, on the back. Turn under the front side of the card, tuck it in under the backing fabric, and stick the batting to the glue/tape. Then turn under the edge of the backing fabric, tuck in the corners, and slip stitch the bottom closed.

Let's Celebrate!

12. Sign the back of your card using the gel pens or markers. Be sure to include the date.
13. If desired, attach plastic rings or pop tops to the back, behind the upper corners of the card, or pin a bar pin in the center of the card. The card also could be framed.

jungle fever pillow

Go on a fabric safari to pick a faux fur print. Add a simple black accent. Then listen for the sound of distant drums as you whip up this jungle-inspired pillow in under an hour!

Difficulty:

DESIGNER

Ann Brouillette

FINISHED SIZE

12" square

MATERIALS

½ yd. of 54" animal print faux fur

¼ yd. black fabric

16" pillow form

CUTTING

From faux fur:

- 1 square 12½" x 12½"
- 2 strips 2½" x 12½"
- 2 strips 2½" x 16½"
- 2 strips 9" x 16½"

From black:

- 4 strips 2" x 12½"
- 2 strips 2½" x 16½"

CONSTRUCTION

1. Press the four 2" x 12½" black strips in half lengthwise, wrong sides together. (The strips now will be 1" x 12½".)
2. Match raw edges of a black folded strip to one side of the 12½" faux fur square, and sew using a ¼" seam. Sew a second black folded strip to the opposite side of the 12½" square, matching raw edges. Now sew the other two strips to the sides of the square in the same way. **Note:** All the folded edges will be loose, facing the center of the 12½" square.
3. Sew the 2½" x 12½" faux fur pieces to the top and bottom edges of the unit you made in step 2. Then sew the 2½" x 16½" pieces to the sides. Press. The pillow front is now finished.
4. Press under ¼" on one long side of a 2½" x 16½" black strip. Match the raw edge of the black strip (the side that's not pressed under) to one side of a 9" x 16½" faux fur strip, right sides together, and stitch using a ¼" seam. Fold the black strip in half to the wrong side, so the pressed edge just covers the stitching line, and topstitch in place. Repeat these steps using the other black strip and faux fur piece. These pieces make up the pillow back.
5. Lay the front of the pillow right side up. Place the two backing pieces, right sides down, on the pillow top, with the black edges in the middle. Match the raw edges of the backing pieces to the outside edges of the pillow front. (The backing pieces will overlap in the middle of the pillow.) Sew ¼" from the edge all the way around the pillow. Trim corners and turn right side out.
6. Insert the pillow form through the overlapping back flaps.

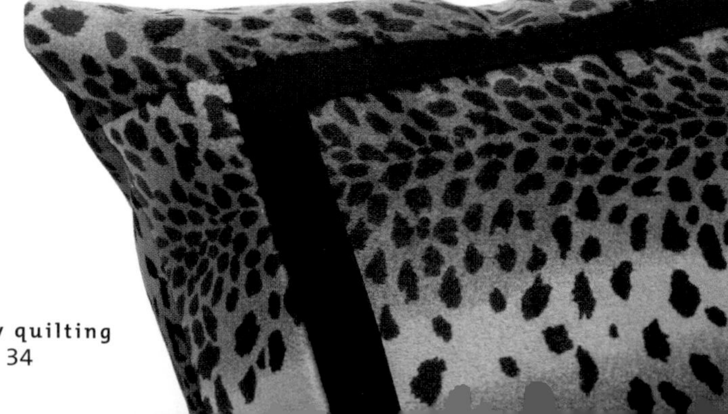

hearts afire quilt

Who says a snuggly, girlie quilt can't have pizzazz? This one mixes slashed electric pink hearts on a whimsical floral background with four-patch blocks in a pink-on-pink leopard print and a yellow-orange check—all from the softest flannels. The rows are quilted during construction to oh-so-huggable polar fleece in red-hot pink and red. Fusible batting makes quilting on the fleece a snap, keeping the fleece smooth and pucker-free while you quilt. And best of all, no binding is required!

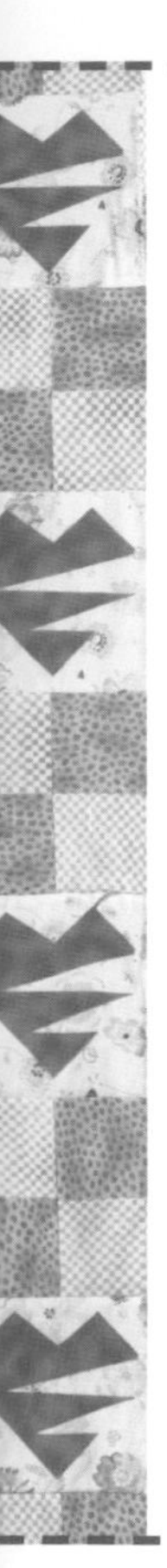

Difficulty:

DESIGNER

Tomme J. Fent

FINISHED SIZE

Approx. 56" x 68"

FINISHED BLOCK SIZE

6" x 6"

MATERIALS

Important: Fabric requirements for flannels are generous to allow for shrinkage. You *must* prewash and machine dry your fabrics before cutting. The flannel will shrink considerably, while the polyester fleece will shrink little, if at all. If you do not prewash, your quilt will distort the first time you wash it, and the fleece will leave fuzzies all over the flannels.

1 1/3 yd. pink-on-pink dotted flannel, for four-patches

1 1/3 yd. yellow-orange checked flannel, for four-patches

1 2/3 yd. mostly white print flannel, for appliqué background

1 1/2 yd. hot pink flannel, for hearts

2 1/2 yd. lightweight fusible webbing (such as Heat'n Bond® Lite Iron-On Adhesive by Therm O Web or Fine Fuse® Fusible Adhesive from Quilters' Resource®). **Note:** Fusible webbings vary in width. This yardage is for 17" webbing. If the webbing you choose is wider, you will need less. Just be sure to get enough to cut 40 squares 5 1/4" x 5 1/4".

2 yd. 100% polyester fleece in hot pink (60" wide), for borders. (Borders are not pieced, so you will have a lot of the border fleece left over to make coordinating pillows or other accents.)

2 yd. 100% polyester fleece in red (60" wide), for backing

1 package June Tailor 100% polyester low-loft Fusible Batting™ (twin size, 72" x 90", or queen, if twin is not available). **Note:** To baste quilt in traditional manner, you may use any low-loft 100% polyester batting. Cotton batting is *not* recommended for this quilt.

The WaveEdge™ Ruler

Monofilament thread

Red thread to match fleece backing

Neutral thread for piecing

CUTTING

- 80 squares 3 1/2" x 3 1/2" of pink-on-pink dotted flannel
- 80 squares 3 1/2" x 3 1/2" of yellow-orange checked flannel
- 40 squares 6 1/2" x 6 1/2" of white flannel background print
- 40 squares 5 1/2" x 5 1/2" of hot pink flannel
- 2 strips 4 1/2" x 66" of hot pink fleece
- 2 strips 4 1/2" x 60" of hot pink fleece
- 40 squares 5 1/4" x 5 1/4" of fusible webbing
- Fusible Batting™, cut to 51" x 63" (Batting does not extend into borders.)

CONSTRUCTION

All seams are sewn using 1/4" seam allowance.

MAKING THE BLOCKS

1. Make the four-patches as follows. Stitch together a square of the pink dotted fabric and a square of the yellow-orange checked fabric, right sides together. Continue,

making 80 pink and yellow-orange pairs. Press all seam allowances toward the pink squares. Join two sets of squares, right sides together, with the pink and yellow-orange squares next to each other. (Fig. 1) Press. Repeat to make 40 four-patch blocks.

2. Trace heart pattern (which has already been reversed) onto the back of each of the 40 squares of fusible webbing. Fuse each 5 1/4" webbing square onto the back of a 5 1/2" hot pink flannel square, following manufacturer's instructions. Cut out hearts on drawn lines.

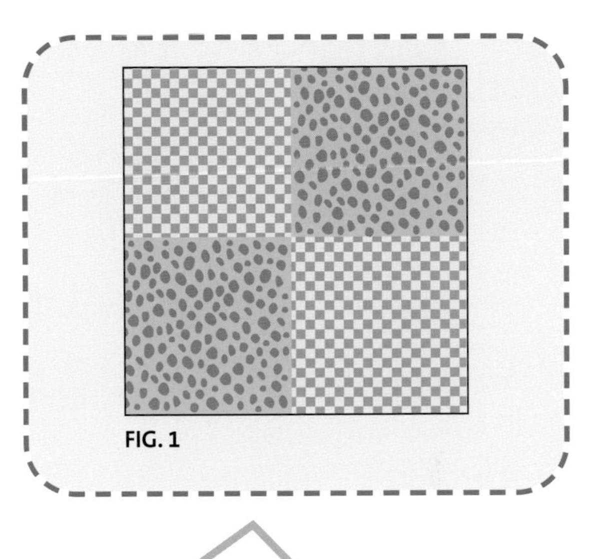
FIG. 1

3. Press all 40 white flannel background print squares in half *very lightly* with right sides together, to create a pressed line; unfold the squares. Position a pink heart on a white background square, lining up the center of the heart with the pressed crease. The bottom and top points of the heart, and each of the sides, should be 3/4" from the outer edges of the background square. Fuse, following manufacturer's instructions.

4. Set up your machine for machine appliqué with monofilament thread, as described in steps 6 and 7 of the instructions for the Let's Celebrate! Fabric Greeting Card (pages 31–32). Appliqué each of the hearts to the background squares. (Fig. 2)

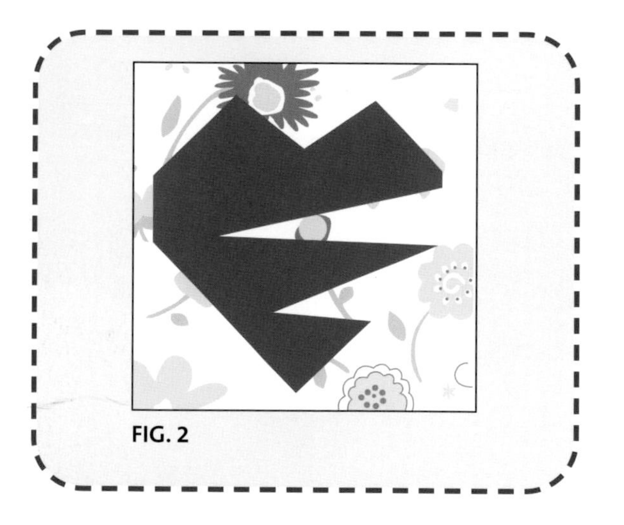

FIG. 2

MAKING THE ROWS

5. Remove monofilament thread from your machine, and thread with neutral piecing thread. Join 4 four-patch blocks to 4 heart blocks, alternating blocks, and *beginning with a four-patch block*. Be sure the pink dotted fabric is always in the upper right and lower left of the four-patch blocks. Press all seams to the *left*. Repeat five times.

6. Join 4 four-patch blocks to 4 heart blocks, alternating blocks, and *beginning with a heart block*. Be sure the pink dotted fabric is always in the upper right and lower left of the four-patch blocks. Press all seams to the *right*. Repeat five times.

PREPARING TO QUILT

7. Find and mark the center (length and width) of the Fusible Batting™. Lay the batting on your ironing board with the center visible. Find and mark the center (length and width) of the red fleece, and lay the fleece on the batting, matching the centers. The red fleece should extend at least 5" past the batting on all sides.

8. Fuse red fleece backing fabric to Fusible Batting™, as follows: Cover your ironing board with an old ironing board cover or old sheet, or turn the cover over to the back side. You will get small amounts of fusible material on your ironing board during this process because you must use steam to get the batting to adhere to the soft fleece (even though the batting packaging will tell you not to use steam in order to fuse batting to only one side of the quilt).

   Use your iron's lowest steam setting, and *do a test* on a small piece of fleece. *If your iron is too hot, it will melt the fleece!* Begin in the center and press outward toward one side; then return to the center and press outward toward the other side. Immediately lift the batting and fleece from the ironing board, before it cools. Repeat, moving from the center up to one end, and then from the center to the other end, until the entire batting piece is fused to the fleece. This is the quilt back.

9. Lay out quilt back, batting side up. Using a yardstick and a pencil, mark a straight line across the center of the quilt back from side to side. Also make a visible mark at the center of the drawn line. Lay quilt back on the ironing board, batting side up, with the drawn line in the center of the ironing board and the center mark visible.

QUILTING ROWS TO THE QUILT BACK

10. Select one row of quilt blocks that begins with a four-patch block. Lay the row right side up across the quilt back, matching the *bottom* of the row to the marked center line on the batting. Match the center of the row of blocks to the center mark on the batting. Using the same steam setting on your iron as before, fuse from the center of the row to the left side, and then from the center to the right side. **Note:** The red fleece will extend several inches beyond each end of the row, and the batting may extend slightly past the end of each row of blocks.

11. Thread your machine with red thread in the top and bobbin. Select a row of blocks that begins with a heart block. Lay this row on top of the row you fused to the quilt, right sides together, matching the raw edges on one long side and matching the seam lines between the blocks. Pin in place. Stitch through all layers, 1/4" from the matched raw edges of the rows. Sew slowly and use a long stitch (3.0 mm). Backstitch at the beginning and end of each row, and do not sew past the ends of the row. Press the newly added row from the front, pressing it up and away from the center row. This will press the seam and fuse the new row at the same time. Check the fleece back to be sure there are no puckers before moving to the next row.

12. Continue adding rows, alternating quilt-block rows that begin with four-patches and hearts, until you reach the top of the quilt. Then go back to the center row, and add rows in the same manner from the center to the bottom of the quilt.

13. When all rows have been sewn to the quilt back, thread your machine with monofilament thread in the top and red in the bobbin, and quilt down each vertical seam line, either in the ditch with a straight stitch, or using a wavy line.

ADDING THE BORDERS

14. Place red thread back in the top of your machine. Using the smaller curves on the WaveEdge™ Ruler, trim one long edge on each of the 4 hot pink fleece border strips. Next, place the strip on the rotary mat with the tops of the curves along the same line. (Fig. 3) Place your rotary ruler with the 4" line on the line where the curves are lined up, and trim the opposite edge to straighten. You now should have a border strip that is 4" at its widest, with one straight edge and one wavy edge.

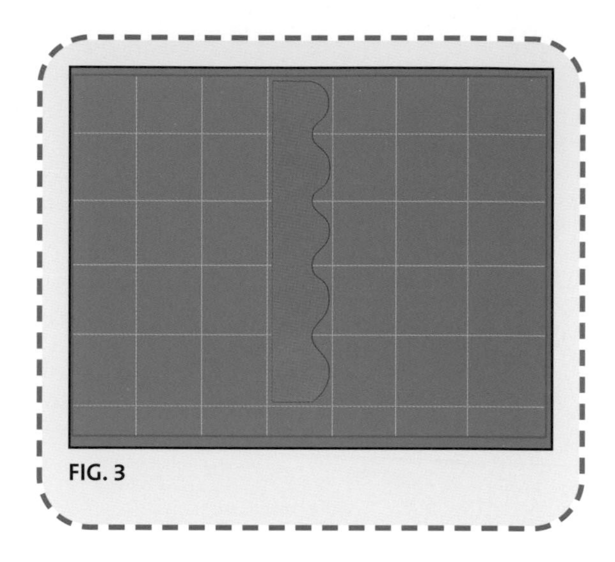

FIG. 3

15. Measure the length of the quilt through the center. Cut the 66" border strips to this length. Find the center of a border strip and mark with a pin. Pin the border strip to one side of the quilt, matching the straight edge of the border strip to the edges of the rows, and the center of the border strip to the center seam line of the quilt. The curved edge should be facing toward the center of the quilt. Stitch through all layers, 1/4" from the straight edge. Backstitch at the beginning and end of the border strip, and don't sew past the ends of the border strip. Repeat to add the other border strip to the opposite side of the quilt. (Fig. 2) Press borders away from quilt center.

16. Measure the width of the quilt through the center, measuring to the outer edge of the curves of the border strips you added in step 15. Cut the 60" border strips to this length. Lay one border strip along the top of the quilt with the curves facing away from the center. Overlap 1/2" of the straight edge of the border strip with the top row of blocks. Use the wavy ruler to trim the sides of the border strip to match the side borders on the quilt. Smooth curves at corners as desired. Then sew the border strip to the top of the quilt, following the instructions in step 15. Repeat for the bottom border. Be sure not to stitch past the ends of the border strips. Press borders away from quilt center.

17. Pin curved outer edges of border strips to red fleece backing fabric. Stitch 1/4" from the curved edge all the way around the quilt.

FINISHING THE QUILT

18. Position the WaveEdge™ Ruler on the red fleece about 1/2" beyond the edge of the hot pink border, matching the curves, and trim on all sides. Smooth curves on corners as desired. No binding is required.

19. Wash your quilt in cold water on gentle cycle to remove the fusible product in the batting. Dry on low temperature.

on the go

Life may seem like a whirlwind, as you rush between home, school, work, parties, weddings, baby showers, doctors' appointments, yoga classes—yikes! These three stylish bags are just the thing to help keep you organized and looking fine. Start with a Wacky Tacky Bag, which you can customize with fabrics and embellishments that show off your unique style. Long days can take their toll, but you'll be able to freshen up anywhere when you carry essential cosmetics and more in the bright Paintbox Makeup Bag. Better yet, it's plastic-lined to protect your purse or backpack from spills. When it's finally time to pamper and rejuvenate yourself with a yoga session, carry your mat in sophisticated style with the Lotus Blossom Yoga Bag.

wacky tacky bag

Go wild with glittery threads, fuzzy yarns, beads, and fancy machine stitches in this quick-to-make crazy-quilted bag. The designer chose African-inspired fabrics and colors for her bag. You can select fabrics and embellishments that reflect your own personality.

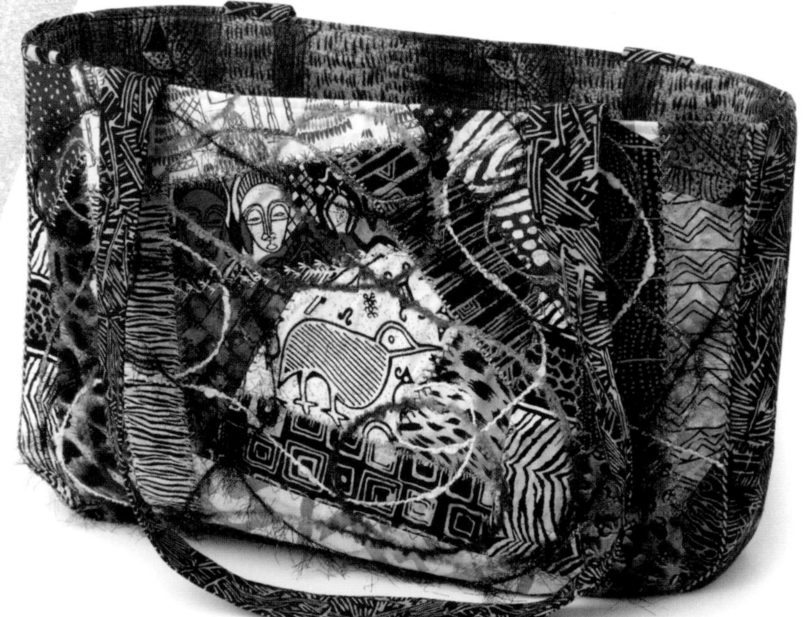

Difficulty:

DESIGNER

Margaret Hunt

FINISHED SIZE

Approx. 13" x 18" x 3"

MATERIALS

For the bag front, select one fabric with a theme, and a variety of fat quarters and scraps to coordinate with the theme fabric. Optional: Include some velvets, glittery fabrics, silk, or lamé for extra pizzazz.

1/2 yd. for back of bag

1 1/3 yd. for gusset and handles (for strips cut on length of grain with no piecing)

2/3 yd. for lining

1/4 yd. for piping, or approx. 3 yd. of purchased drapery cord or ready-made piping

1 1/2 yd. of heavy, iron-on craft backing such as Timtex™ interfacing (22" wide) or Pellon® Decor-Bond® (44" wide)

Threads to match and contrast

Monofilament thread for couching

Piping or zipper foot, free-motion foot, and regular sewing foot

Embellishments: These are optional, and you won't need all of them. Choose from beads and buttons, rayon and metallic threads and filaments, and a variety of yarns—anything you think would look good on your bag.

CUTTING

1. From heavy craft backing:
- 2 rectangles 14" x 18"
- 1 strip 4" x 46 1/2"
- 2 strips 3 1/2" x 25"
2. From backing fabric:
- 1 rectangle 14" x 18"
3. From gusset and handle fabric:
- 1 strip 4" x 46 1/2"
- 2 strips 3 1/2" x 25"
4. From lining fabric:
- 1 rectangle 18 1/2" x 31 1/2"
5. From theme fabric:
- 1 five-sided piece 4" to 5" wide and high

quilt wise

Your bag will be more interesting if you cut the theme fabric piece with sides of uneven lengths.

6. From remaining fabrics:
- Several 2" and 3" strips (Strips don't have to be cut evenly. For example, a strip could be 3" wide at one end and 2" wide at the other.)

CONSTRUCTION

PIECING THE BAG FRONT

The bag front is pieced by using the heavy craft backing as a foundation, and stitching pieces of fabric to it using the flip-and-sew technique. Place the five-sided piece of your theme fabric, right side up, in the center of one of the 14" x 18" rectangles of heavy craft backing, and secure with a pin. Select one of the fabric strips and place it face down on top of the five-sided fabric, matching one edge. Stitch through all three layers with a 1/4" seam, stopping when you reach the end of the theme fabric. Flip the strip up and finger press the seam.

Add a second strip to the next edge. Trim the first strip at the seam line of the second strip. Continue adding strips clockwise around the center. (See Figs. 1–5) Keep adding strips

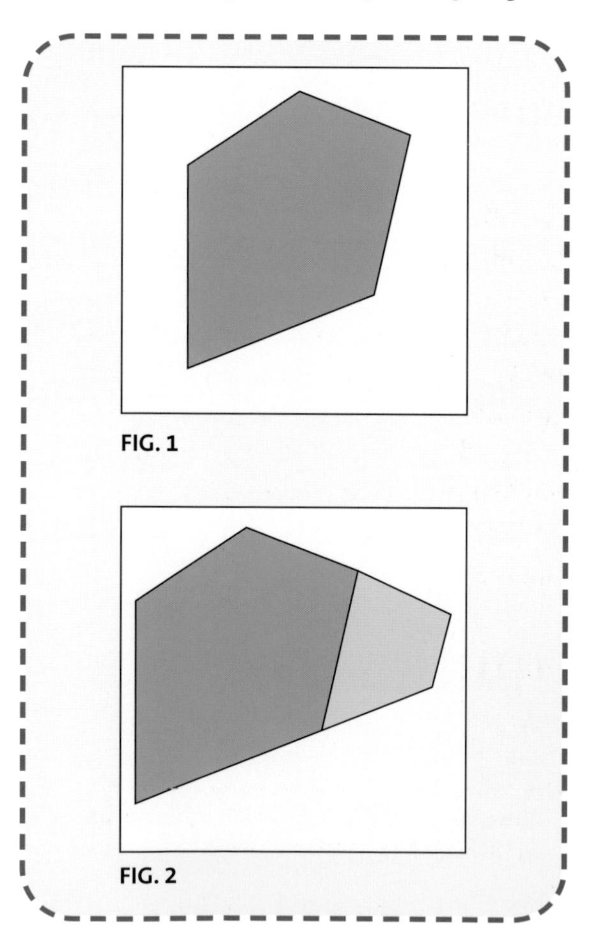

FIG. 1

FIG. 2

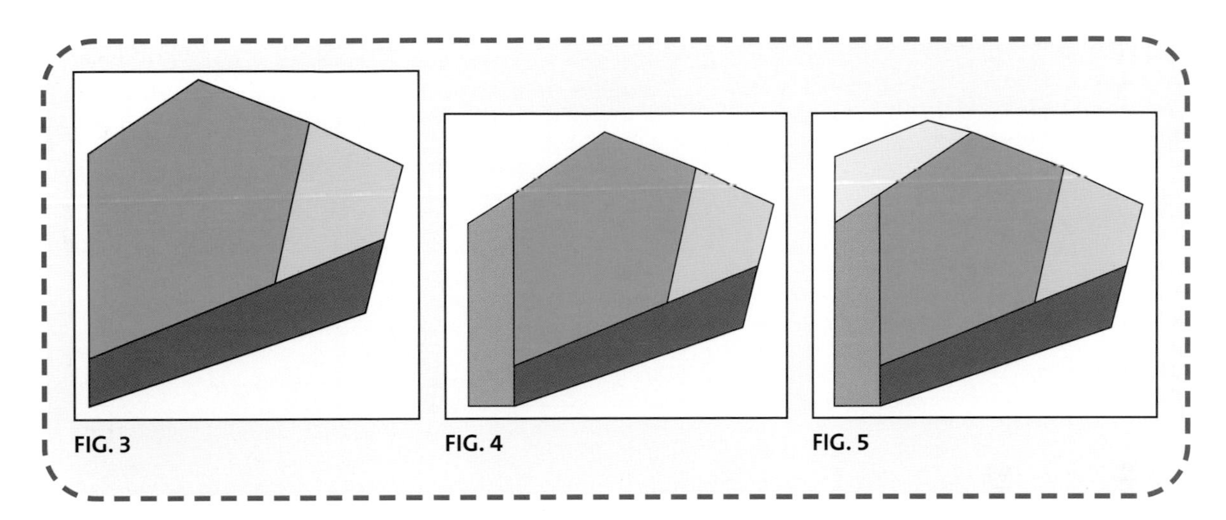
FIG. 3 FIG. 4 FIG. 5

until you have covered the entire rectangle. Trim rectangle to original size (14" x 18"), so no fabric extends over the edges. Baste 1/8" from edge all the way around the rectangle, and press the bag front.

ADDING EMBELLISHMENTS

Embellish your bag as desired. To **couch yarns** (attaching decorative yarns by stitching), use your free-motion foot and monofilament thread, and zigzag the yarns in place. Hairy yarns can be zigzagged by brushing the hairs to one side as you sew. You can add **machine embroidery** using specialty stitches on your machine or free-motion stitching.

Add beads and buttons, if desired.

quilt wise

For added interest when you machine embroider, use two threads of matching or coordinating colors at the same time. Just thread your machine so that *both* threads go through the needle together.

TRIMMING CORNERS, ADDING PIPING, AND ATTACHING GUSSET

Trim off *two* corners on one long side of the rectangle. To do this, mark a spot 1 1/2" from the corner on the bottom and 1 1/2" from the corner up the side of the rectangle. Then cut on the diagonal from mark to mark. (Fig. 6) *Be sure to cut both corners on the same long side of the rectangle!*

Add piping 1/4" from the sides and bottom of the bag, including around the cut corners.

Iron the 4" x 46 1/2" strip of heavy craft backing to the wrong side of the 4" x 46 1/2" strip of gusset fabric. Place the gusset fabric right sides together with the bag front, and stitch around sides and bottom using a scant 1/4" seam (just outside the piping) and a short stitch length (2 mm).

MAKING THE BACK

Fuse the remaining 14" x 18" rectangle of heavy craft backing to the wrong side of the 14" x 18" rectangle of backing fabric. Trim corners of one long side at the same angle as

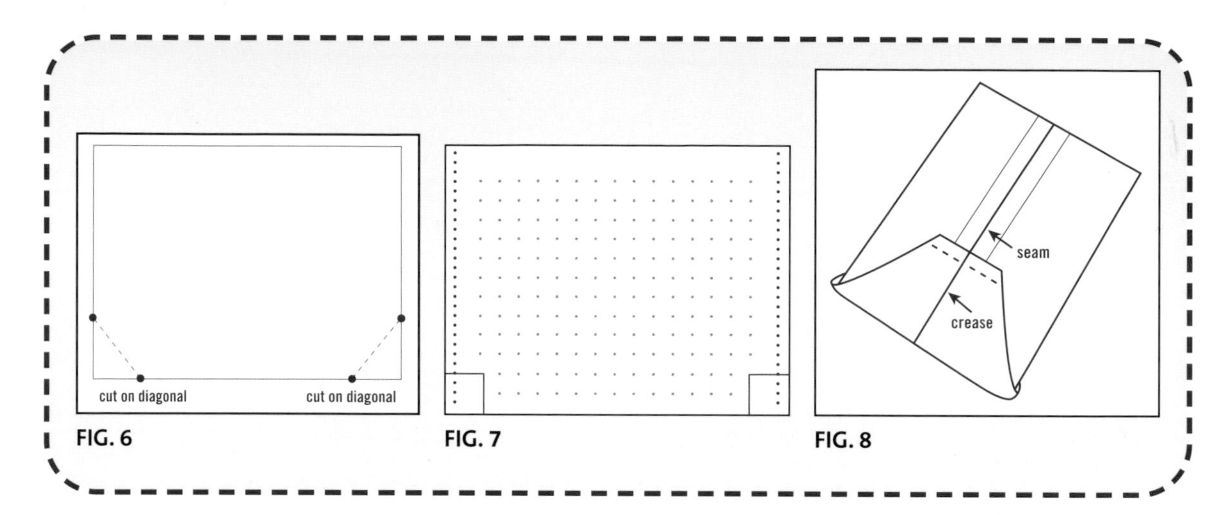

FIG. 6 FIG. 7 FIG. 8

on the front. (Fig. 6) Place the back right sides together with the raw edge of the gusset, and stitch around the sides and bottom using a 1/4" seam. *Be sure you stitch the side with the cut corners to the gusset.*

ADDING THE HANDLES

Iron the two 3 1/2" x 25" strips of heavy craft backing to the wrong sides of the two 3 1/2" x 25" strips of handle fabric. Fold the handles lengthwise, right sides together, and stitch down the long edge and across one end using a 1/4" seam, making a tube. Turn the tube right side out, and cut off the short end just inside the seam line. (It's easier to turn the tubes if you sew across one end of the tube. The end is then trimmed off after the tube is turned.)

On the top edge of the bag front, measure in 2" from each side seam and mark with a pin. On the outside of the bag front, pin the ends of one handle strip at the marked points, matching the raw edges of the handle strip to the raw edges of the bag. (The handle will be hanging down from the top of the bag.) Stitch *securely* using a 1/4" seam. Attach the other handle to the back of the bag, using the same measurements (2" from each side seam). Press handles up and away from the bag. At the same time, fold down the top raw edge of the bag 1/2", and press all the way around the bag.

ADDING THE LINING

With right sides together, fold the 18 1/2" x 31 1/2" rectangle of lining in half (so it's 18 1/2" x 15 3/4"), and stitch the sides using a 1/4" seam. Press the lining flat, to form a crease along the bottom edge. Cut a 2" square from each of the bottom corners of the lining. (Fig. 7) With right sides together, line up the raw edges, matching the crease in the lining bottom to the side seam. Stitch 1/4" from the edge. (Fig. 8)

Turn under and press the lining 1/2" from the raw edge all the way around the top. Insert lining into bag, wrong sides together, matching side seams. Pin lining to bag, with top edge of lining slightly below top edge of bag. Sew lining in place, stitching right at the edge of the lining, using monofilament thread.

Enjoy your Wacky Tacky Bag!

paintbox makeup bag

Every woman needs a special "paintbox" to carry those essential cosmetics and other toiletries. This one is lined with plastic to protect your purse from accidental spills. The bag is so quick and easy, you can make several to give as gifts. Your friends are sure to want one!

Difficulty:

DESIGNER

Tomme J. Fent

FINISHED SIZE

Approx. 5" x 7½"

MATERIALS

3 rectangles 6" x 8" of red fabric, for back of bag and lining

2" strips of 6 bright colors, for front of bag

2 rectangles 6" x 8" of batting

2 rectangles 6" x 8" of vinyl (The softer, slightly opaque vinyl works better than the totally clear vinyl. The clear vinyl tends to stick together and is difficult to sew by machine, and it will make your bag stiffer.)

7" red zipper

Red thread

CONSTRUCTION

1. Thread machine with red thread in top and bobbin. Layer one rectangle of batting between 2 rectangles of red fabric, with wrong sides of fabric against batting. Stitch through all three layers on a diagonal line from corner to corner. Stitch 2 lines on each side of center line, with stitching lines 2" apart. (Fig. 1) Trim to even up the sides and return the rectangle to 6" x 8". This is the bag back.
2. Layer the other rectangle of batting on top of the wrong side of the remaining rectangle of red fabric. Select one 2" strip of fabric, and lay the strip face up on top of batting diagonally from corner to corner. One edge of the fabric should overlap the diagonal by 1/4" so that you'll be stitching on the diagonal. (Fig. 2) Don't worry; even if it's not perfectly lined up, it will look fine.
3. Select a second 2" strip of fabric, and lay it face down on the first strip (so the strips are right sides together), matching the edges. Stitch through all layers 1/4" from the matched edges of the strips. Flip the top strip up and press away from the first strip.
4. Select a third 2" strip of fabric, and sew it to the second strip as above. Then add strips on the other side of the first strip in the same manner. Press after adding each strip.
5. Turn the rectangle over so you can see the red fabric. Using the red rectangle as a guide, trim to return the rectangle to 6" x 8". The strip-pieced unit is the bag front.

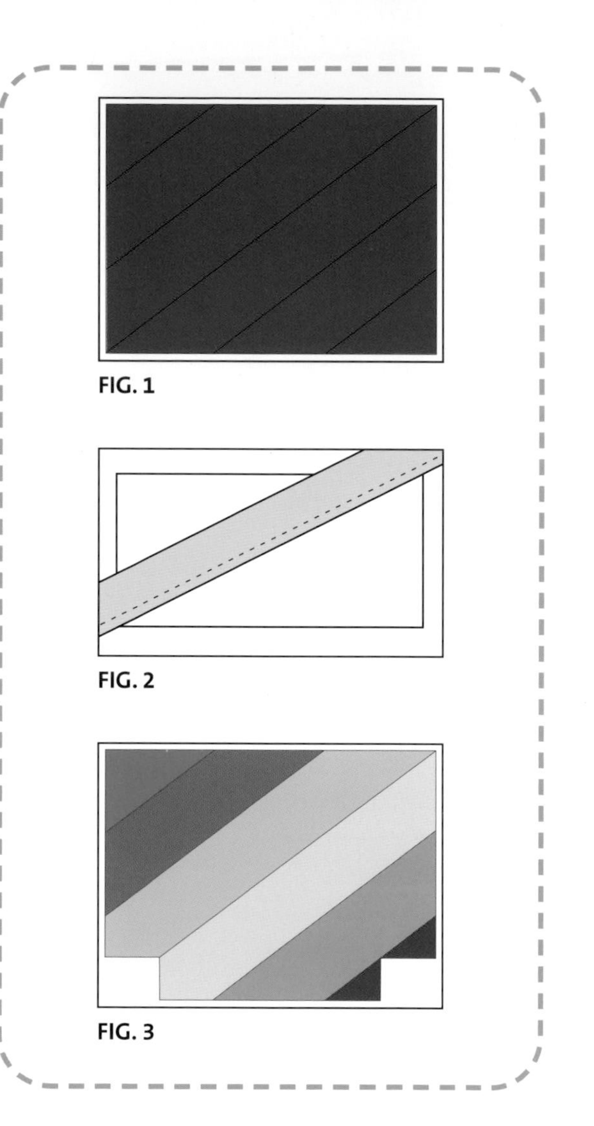
FIG. 1

FIG. 2

FIG. 3

6. Place one vinyl rectangle on the back of each quilted unit. Baste, matching edges.
7. Cut out a 1" square from two corners on the long side of each rectangle. (Fig. 3)
8. Pin the zipper facedown on top of bag front, with edge of zipper tape matching top of bag front, and zipper pull facing left. The zipper pull should be slightly more than 1/4" from the left edge of the bag

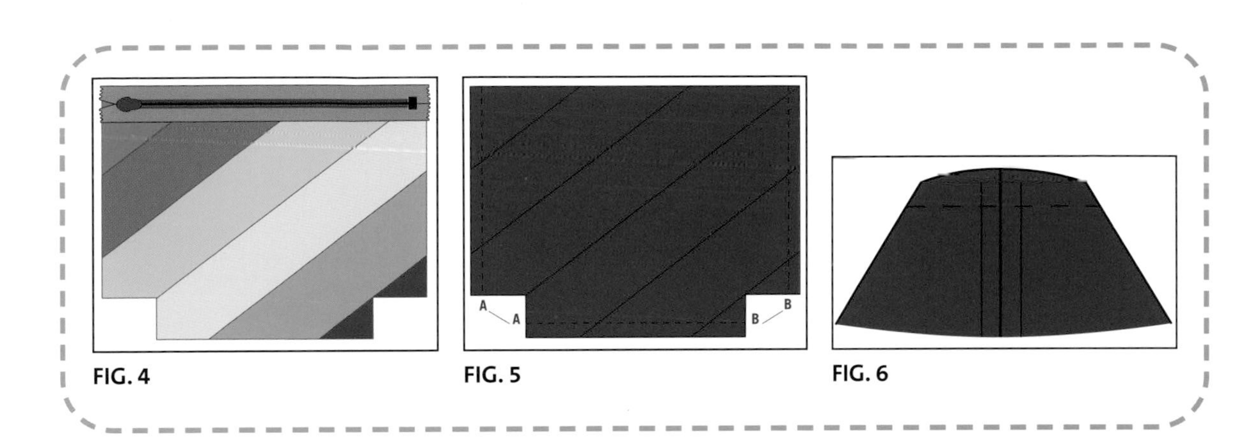

FIG. 4 FIG. 5 FIG. 6

front. (Fig. 4) Stitch 3/16" to 1/4" from center of zipper. (You will have to open the zipper partially to stitch at the beginning of the zipper. Then, with the needle down, lift the presser foot to close the zipper, and continue stitching to the end of the zipper.)

do it right: This step is easier if you use your machine's zipper foot. As an alternative, use a zigzag foot, and move the needle over to the far left so you can stitch without the foot having to travel over the top of the zipper.

9. Flip the zipper up so it's facing away from the bag front. Topstitch 1/8" to 1/4" from the top edge of the bag top.
10. Lay the bag back facedown on top of the bag front, lining up the sides, and pin the top of the bag back to the other raw edge of the zipper. Turn over so you can see the zipper, and stitch as above. Flip bag back up so it extends away from the zipper. (The zipper will be in the middle, with the bag front extending to one side and the bag back extending to the other side of the zipper.) Topstitch.
11. Flip bag back down, right sides together with bag front. Stitch sides using 1/4" seam and short stitch (2.0 mm), stopping at the cut-out square. (Fig. 5)
12. Put your hand up inside the bag and *open the zipper!* (You will turn the bag through the zipper opening when complete.) Then stitch the bottom edges together. (Fig. 5)
13. Look at Fig. 5, and note the location of the As and Bs, at the bottom and side seams. Match As and sew a straight seam 1/4" from the short edge. (Fig. 6) Match Bs and repeat.
14. Turn bag right side out through zipper opening.

lotus blossom yoga bag

Carry your yoga mat in style with this sturdy, serene bag that features paper-pieced lotus blossoms and beautiful batik fabrics. The bag works with all standard-size yoga mats.

Difficulty:

DESIGNER

Janice Cook

FINISHED SIZE

Approx. 6" x 6" x 26"

MATERIALS

5 fat quarters (18" x 22") of assorted batiks in coordinating colors

1 yd. fabric for bag and strap

½ yd. fabric for lining

1⅔ yd. of 1" strapping

18" draw cord and cord stopper

CUTTING

For Lotus Blossom Blocks

Cut from the batiks:

- 3 squares 2" x 2" for section 1 of blocks
- 3 squares 2" x 2" for blossoms
- 3 squares 2" x 2" for section 2 of blocks
- 3 rectangles 1½" x 3" for section 3 of blocks
- 3 rectangles 2" x 2½" for section 4 of blocks
- 3 rectangles 2" x 3½" for section 5 of blocks
- 6 squares 4" x 4", cut in half on diagonal, for sections 6, 7, 8, and 9 of blocks

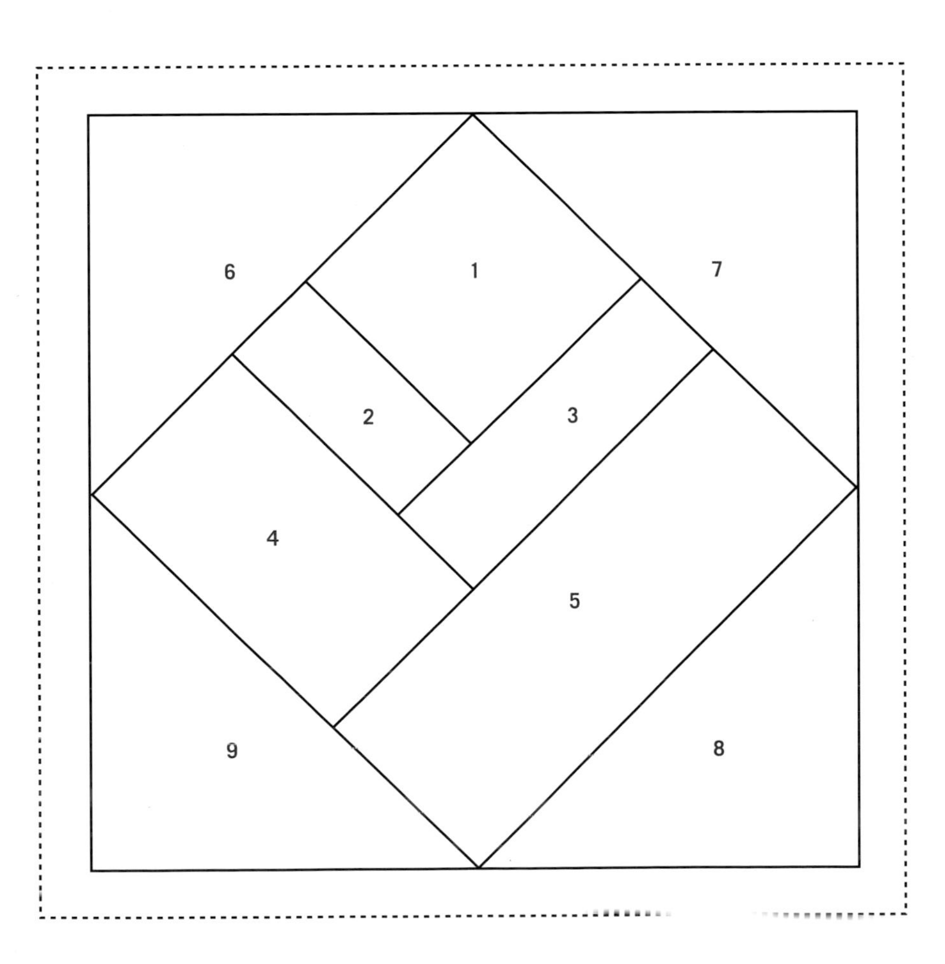

For Center Panel

Cut from the bag fabric:

- 2 strips $2\frac{1}{2}$" x $4\frac{1}{2}$"
- 1 rectangle $4\frac{1}{2}$" x $8\frac{1}{2}$"
- 1 rectangle $4\frac{1}{2}$" x $6\frac{1}{2}$"

For Bag

- 2 strips 3" wide by length of fabric, for strap
- 1 rectangle 13" x 30"
- 6" circle
- 1 rectangle $17\frac{1}{2}$" x 30" from lining fabric
- 6" circle from lining fabric

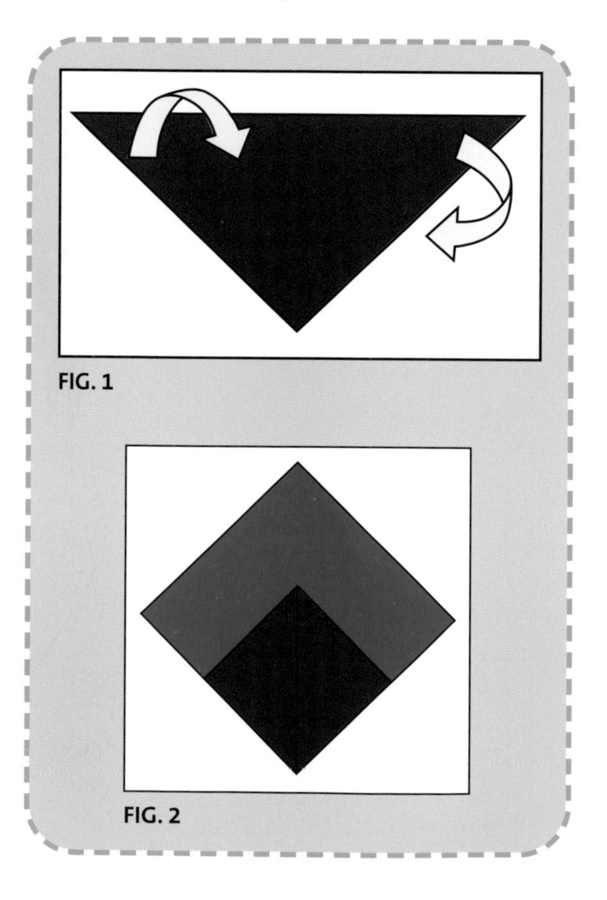

FIG. 1

FIG. 2

CONSTRUCTION

MAKING THE LOTUS BLOSSOM BLOCK

do it right: When doing paper piecing, it's best to use a shortened stitch length (1.5 mm) and a larger needle to make the paper easier to remove after piecing.

1. Copy the paper piecing pattern three times, once for each block.
2. Fold the 2" blossom square in half diagonally to make a triangle. Press. Fold the two corners on the long side down to meet the point, forming a 1" square. (Fig. 1) Spray heavily with spray starch and press.
3. Place a section 1 square right side up on the wrong (unlined) side of the pattern (so the wrong side of the fabric faces the wrong side of the paper pattern). Position the piece so the edges extend exactly $\frac{1}{4}$" into sections 2 and 3 of the pattern.

   do it right: Hold the pattern and fabric up to a light source to see if the fabric is positioned correctly. Pin the fabric in place on the right (lined) side of the pattern, making sure the pin doesn't cross over the line between sections 1 and 2.

4. Place the lotus blossom, folded side up, on top of the section 1 square, lining up the raw edges of the blossom with the lower edges of the section 1 piece (the edges that extend into sections 2 and 3). (Fig. 2)

5. Place a section 2 square right sides together with the section 1 square and the blossom, lining up the lower edges. Pin in place. Turn pattern over and sew on the line between sections 1 and 2.

   Flip the section 2 piece away from the section 1 piece, and press open. Repeat these steps to add the section 3 piece over section 3 of the pattern.

   do it right: When paper piecing, always start and stop 2 or 3 stitches before and after the drawn line.

6. From the right side of the pattern, lay a postcard on top of sections 1 and 2, along the line between sections 2 and 4, and fold back the pattern along this line. This will expose the excess fabric beyond the seam line. Trim the excess fabric 1/4" from the paper fold. Be sure you don't cut the seam allowance off *at* the fold; you must leave a 1/4" seam allowance beyond the fold.

   do it right: An Add-a-Quarter Ruler™ is invaluable for this step. It's a must-have tool if you plan to do much paper piecing.

7. Open the paper pattern flat. Align the rectangle for section 4 along the trimmed edge of the section 2 fabric. Sew along the line between sections 2 and 4 from the right side of the paper, as you did in step 5. Press fabric open.

8. Repeat the process in steps 6 and 7 for the remaining sections of the block, adding fabric in the correct numbered sequence to sections 5, 6, 7, 8, and 9. Make the other two Lotus Blossom blocks in the same manner.

9. Trim the block on the dotted outside line (leaving 1/4" seam allowance beyond the inner, solid line). *Don't remove the paper yet*; leave it in place until the block is sewn into the center panel, then remove the paper.

MAKING THE CENTER PANEL

All seams use 1/4" seam allowance.

1. Sew the 4 1/2" x 8 1/2" rectangle to the top of one Lotus Blossom block.

2. Sew a 2 1/2" x 4 1/2" rectangle to the bottom of the same Lotus Blossom block.

3. Sew a second Lotus Blossom block to the bottom of the 2 1/2" x 4 1/2" rectangle.

4. Sew the other 2 1/2" x 4 1/2" rectangle to the bottom of the second Lotus Blossom block.

5. Sew the third Lotus Blossom block to the bottom of the panel.

6. Sew the 4 1/2" x 6 1/2" rectangle to the bottom of the third Lotus Blossom block.

   You have now completed the center panel. The 8 1/2" section goes at the top of the bag, and the 6 1/2" section goes at the bottom.

MAKING THE BAG

All seams use 1⁄4" seam allowance.

1. Place the 13" x 30" rectangle right sides together with one side of the center panel. Sew, beginning the seam 3" down from the top of the bag, to leave room for the draw cord. (Remember, the 8 1⁄2" section is at the top of the center panel.) Press seam open, and continue pressing all the way to the top so that the 1⁄4" seam allowance on both sides of the 3" opening is also pressed under.
2. With right sides together, sew the other side of the center panel to the 13" x 30" rectangle, this time sewing all the way to the top of the bag. Press seam toward the bag. *Do not turn the bag right side out yet.*
3. Fold the lining rectangle in half lengthwise, right sides together (so it's now 8 3⁄4" x 30"). Sew down the long side beginning 3" from one end. Press seam open, and continue pressing to the top so the 1⁄4" seam allowance on both sides of the 3" opening is also pressed under.
4. Turn lining right side out and slip it over the wrong side of the bag. (The wrong sides should be facing each other.) Match the pressed-under edges at the 3" opening on the bag and the lining, and topstitch them together, sewing across the seam at the bottom of the opening.
5. Machine baste raw edges together at the top and bottom of the bag, 1⁄4" from edge.

MAKING THE STRAP

1. Sew the 3" strips of fabric together and cut to measure 60" long. Press under 1⁄4" down one long side of the 60" strip.
2. Fold under 1⁄4" on one short end of the strap and press. Fold under another 1⁄4" and topstitch down. This is the top of the strap.
3. Lay strapping in the center of the fabric, and fold the unpressed, raw edge of the fabric over the length of the strapping. Fold the pressed edge of the fabric over the raw

edge, and topstitch close to the pressed edge through all layers to hold in place. Topstitch a second line 1/4" from the first stitching line.

MAKING THE DRAW CORD CLOSURE

1. Press under 1/2" on the top edge of the bag (folding fabric down toward the lining).
2. Fold down another 1" (to the top of the opening in the side seam), and press all the way around. Topstitch in place.
3. Thread the draw cord through the casing formed in step 2, and secure with the cord stop.

FINISHING THE BAG

1. Machine baste the 6" circle of bag fabric to the 6" circle of lining fabric, wrong sides together, 1/4" from edge.
2. To attach the strap, center the strap opposite the center panel and about 2" below the draw cord casing. Stitch the top of the strap to the bag using a large X to secure the strap in place. (Fig. 3)

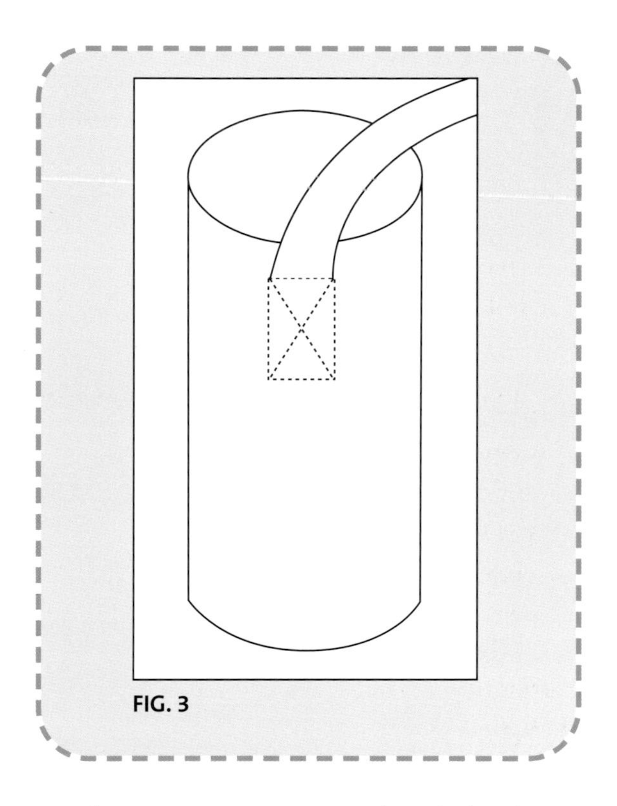

FIG. 3

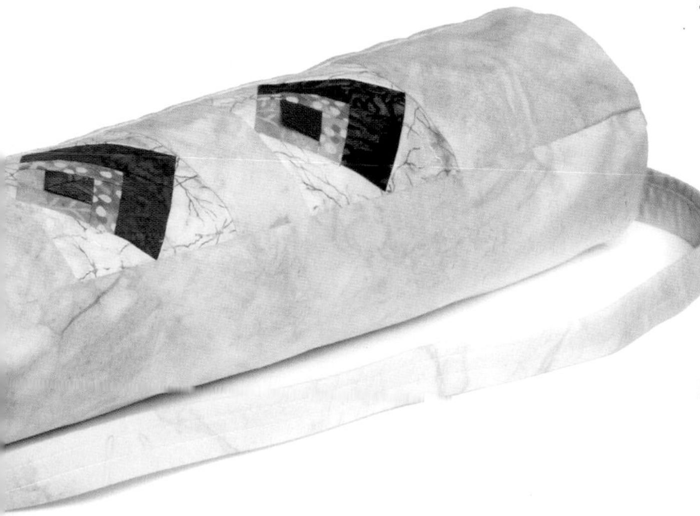

3. If necessary, cut strap to a length that is comfortable for you. Baste the bottom end of the strap to the bottom edge of the bag, making sure the strap hangs down in a straight line from the top of the bag.
4. Clip the bottom edge of the bag to, but not through, the basting. With right sides together, pin the 6" circle section to the bottom of the bag, evenly spacing the bulk. (The lining side of the 6" circle should be facing out, and the fabric side of the circle should be facing into the bag.) Stitch, making sure to catch the end of the strap in your stitching. Stitch again on top of the first stitching.
5. Turn the bag right side out, and you're finished!

just having fun

Sometimes you're feeling creative but don't have the time for a long, involved project. These four designs are just the thing for a relaxing afternoon filled with color and texture. In Cirque de Fabrique, discover how scraps from favorite clothes, leftovers from other projects, and found objects can combine to make a lighthearted wall hanging. When you see a row of traditional Christmas stockings hanging by a fireplace, do you ever wish yours could be as sassy and unique as you are? Try on the Quirky Quilter's Christmas Stocking for size. Maybe you just feel like doodling. Instead of picking up a pencil, doodle in fabric on a Free-Form Fun Pillow. Or experiment with a photo transfer technique that'll turn a child's artwork (or maybe your own) into a Mini Masterpiece.

cirque de fabrique wall hanging

CIRQUE DE FABRIQUE MADE BY EITHNE TAAFFE, QUILTED BY ELAINE KOSNAC

Gather up your scraps and make this simple but striking geometric wall hanging, which combines appliqué, prairie points, buttons, pom-poms, and even ponytail holders in a circus of fabric!

Difficulty:

DESIGNER

Eithne Taaffe

FINISHED SIZE

30" x 30"

MATERIALS

The photo quilt uses fabric scraps from dressmaking, quilting, and assorted old clothes. Don't be limited by our color choices; where the photo quilt uses two shades of yellow, you may decide to use two shades of red. Use scraps you have on hand, or spend a buck or two at a thrift store on a garment to cut up for the project. Look for fun embellishments like beads, buttons, and all things fuzzy and shiny! Any combination of colors and fabrics will work.

You will need six colors, and we give you the fabric requirements for each of them. In parentheses, we tell you where each fabric is located in the photo quilt. Fabric requirements are generous to be sure you have enough to square up the edges before cutting.

Color #1: ½ yd. (yellow satin in top border, corners around center diamond, and long strip below the center)

Color #2: 1 fat quarter (18" x 22") or ⅓ yd. of full-width fabric (textured yellow satin on each side of the center diamond)

Color #3: ⅔ yd. (green)

Color #4: ½ yd. (pink satin)

Color #5: ¼ yd. (bright blue)

Color #6: 1 strip 3" x 26" (purple)

CUTTING

Color #1: Cut a 5½" strip across the width of the fabric.

- From the 5½" strip, cut 4 squares 5½" x 5½".
- Trim the rest of the 5½" strip down to 5" wide (cutting off ½").
- From the 5" strip, cut 3 squares 5" x 5".
- Cut a 2½" strip across the width of the fabric.
- From the 2½" strip, cut 7 squares 2½" x 2½".
- Cut 1 strip 3½" x 30½".

Color #2: 2 squares 10½" x 10½"

Color #3: 8 squares 5" x 5"

- 3 squares 10" x 10"
- 1 strip 2½" x 30½"

Color #4: Cut a 10½" strip across the width of the fabric.

- From the 10½" strip, cut 1 square 10½" x 10½".
- From the rest of the 10½" strip, cut off one 2½" strip.
- From the 2½" strip, cut 8 squares 2½" x 2½" and 3 rectangles 2½" x 4½".
- Cut 1 strip 1½" x 30½".

Color #5: 1 strip 3½" x 28½"

- 8 strips 2½" x 4½"

Color #6: Trim strip to 2½" wide.

- From the strip, cut 4 pieces 2½" x 4½".
- Trim remaining strip down to 1" wide.
- From the 1" strip, cut 2 pieces 1" x 3½".

CONSTRUCTION

Refer to the photo quilt for fabric placement. Use 1/4" seams for piecing.

1. To create the top border, sew together the eight 2 1/2" squares of Color #4 and the seven 2 1/2" squares of Color #1, alternating colors, and beginning and ending with Color #4. Press seams open.
2. To make the prairie points at the top, use the eight 5" squares of Color #3. Fold the square in half diagonally, point to point, to make a triangle. Press. Then fold the triangle in half again to make a smaller triangle. Press. (Figs. 1–3)
3. Sew one of the 1" x 3 1/2" Color #6 strips to each end of the 3 1/2" x 28 1/2" Color #5 strip. Place this strip (which is now 30 1/2" long) right side up, and place the prairie points from step 2 on the strip, aligning the raw edges of the prairie points with one side of the strip. Make sure the open sides of all 8 prairie points are facing in the same direction. Overlap the prairie points by slipping the edge of one point inside the fold of the point next to it, and space the points evenly across the full 30 1/2" width of the Color #5 strip. Pin in place. (Fig. 4)
4. Place the pieced strip from step 1 right side down along the edge where you pinned the prairie points, creating a sandwich with the prairie points in the middle. Pin in place and sew together. Press seam toward the Color #5 strip.

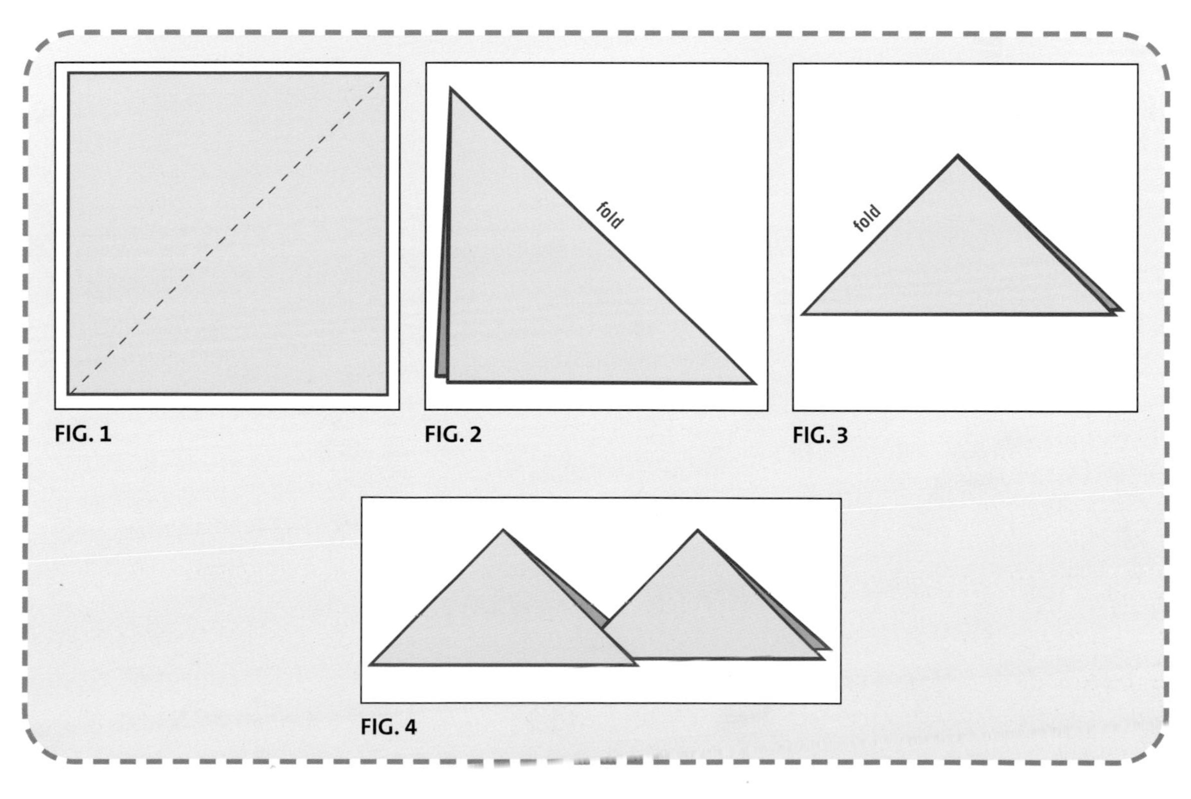

FIG. 1 FIG. 2 FIG. 3 FIG. 4

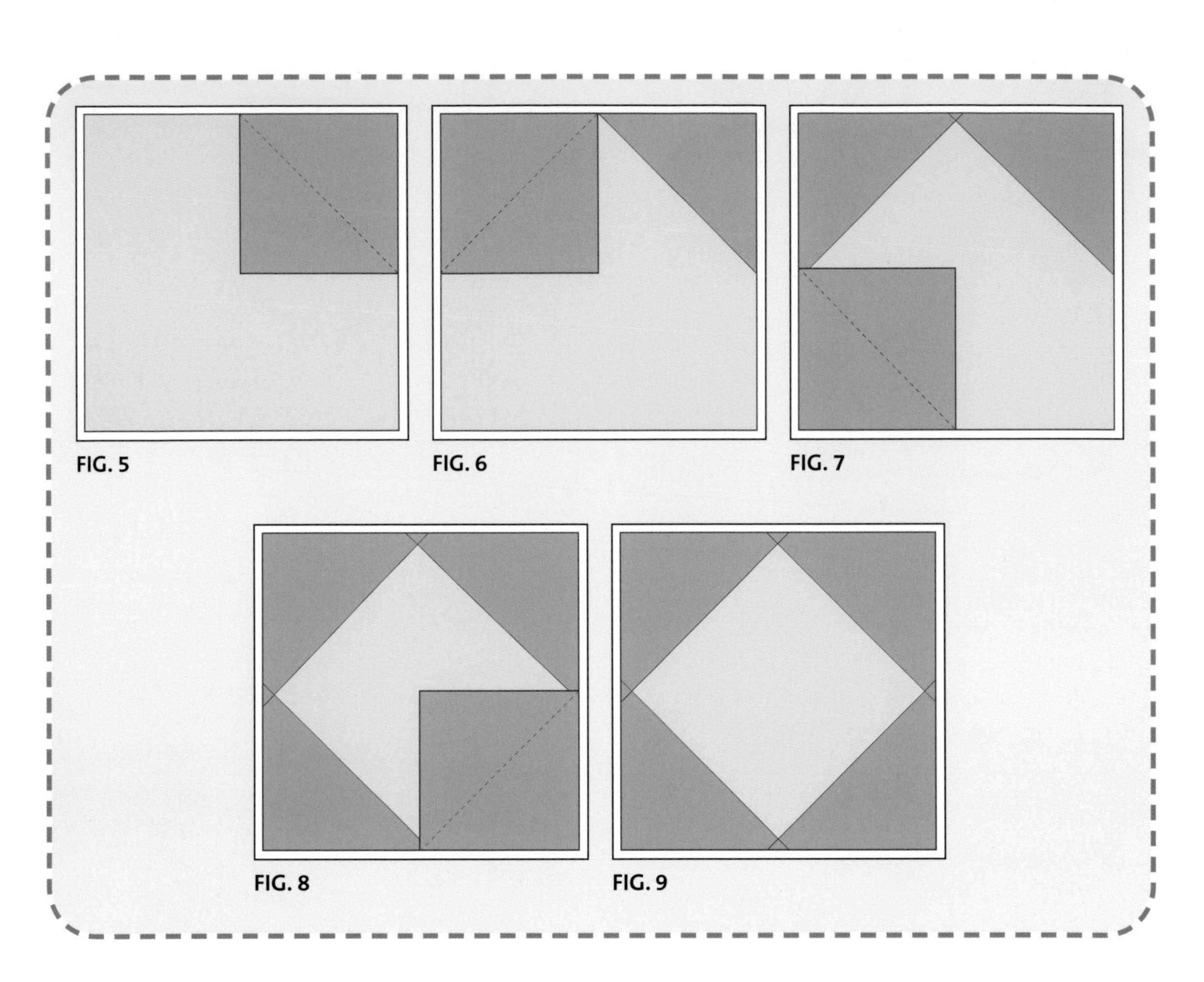

5. The center diamond is made using the flip-and-sew method. Place the $10^1/_2$" Color #4 square right side up. Align one of the $5^1/_2$" Color #1 squares with one corner of the Color #4 square, right side down. Sew a diagonal line from corner to corner of the $5^1/_2$" square. (Fig. 5) Flip the triangle up and press. Repeat on the other three corners, flipping up and pressing each corner as you go. (Figs. 6–9)
6. Sew one $10^1/_2$" Color #2 square on each side of the diamond from step 5, right sides together. Press seams away from the center.
7. Sew the upper border to the center diamond unit with the Color #5 strip next to the diamond unit. (See quilt photo.) Press seam toward the Color #5 strip.
8. Sew together the $2^1/_2$" x $30^1/_2$" Color #3 strip, the $1^1/_2$" x $30^1/_2$" Color #4 strip, and the $3^1/_2$" x $30^1/_2$" Color #1 strip (in that order). Sew the strip unit to the center diamond unit with the Color #3 strip next to the diamond unit. (See quilt photo.) Press seams down (away from center).

9. To create the bottom border, sew together the 2 1/2" x 4 1/2" strips of Colors 4, 5, and 6, along the long edges, in this order: 5-6-5-4-5-6-5-4-5-6-5-4-5-6-5.

   do it right: To keep the seams straight, it's easiest to create three sets of four strips each (5-6-5-4) and one set of three strips (5-6-5), and then sew the four sets together. If you do this, be sure to sew the correct ends of the strips together!

   Press seams open.

10. For the bottom prairie points, use the three 10" Color #3 squares for the large points and the three 5" Color #1 squares for the small points. Follow the directions in step 2 to make the prairie points. Place the small Color #1 points in the center of the larger Color #3 points, aligning raw edges, and pin in place.

11. Place the three large prairie points on the pieced strip from step 9, right sides together. One point should be in the center of the strip, and the other two points should be on the ends of the strip. Pin in place, sew, and iron the seam allowance toward the pieced strip.

12. Sew the bottom of the quilt to the top of the quilt, right sides together, as shown in the photo. Press seam toward the top of the quilt.

13. Place quilt right side up on top of batting. Place backing fabric right side down on top of quilt. On the bottom edge, the backing fabric should extend 1/4" past the seam that joins the large prairie points to the pieced strip. Pin all three layers together. Stitch around top and sides, stopping 1/2" from bottom of backing fabric. Turn right side out and press. Turn backing fabric under 1/2" and press. Hand-stitch lower edge of backing fabric to quilt along seam line that joins the large prairie points to the pieced lower border.

14. Quilt as desired, embellish, and add a hanging sleeve (see Be a Show-off on page 17) and a label.

EMBELLISHMENTS

This quilt can be embellished in any quirky way you choose, with found objects, beads, buttons, charms, and so on. For the photo quilt, we used beads, buttons, ponytail holders, and a pom-pom. Two furry, sparkly ponytail holders were hand sewn on the sides of the center diamond. Buttons were sewn in the centers of the small prairie points at the bottom. The pom-pom was sewn to dangle from the bottom prairie point. Two 1" squares of contrasting fabric were cut and secured to the Color #3 strip under the center diamond using yellow buttons, leaving edges of the fabric squares raw. Four buttons were sewn inside the center diamond to emphasize the shape. Several beads were sewn randomly on the Color #5 strip at the top of the quilt.

Use your imagination—and have fun!

quirky quilter's christmas stocking

A Quirky Quilter needs an out-of-the-ordinary Christmas stocking. This one uses a piece of an antique quilt (made by the designer's grandmother), two pieces of felt, and lots of vintage buttons. It couldn't be easier. Use colors and embellishments to suit your taste and make your own special keepsake. If you don't have a piece of antique quilt, not to worry: we've provided instructions on how to make your own mini-quilt for the stocking's cuff.

Difficulty:

DESIGNER

Nina Gilliland

MATERIALS

Enough felt for two pieces approx. 15" x 18" each. You can use the same color for both the front and back of the stocking, or two different colors.

One 5½" x 17½" piece taken from the edge of an old quilt for the cuff (or see page 66 to make your own cuff)

One 2½" x 7" piece of old quilt for the hanging tab (or a 7" piece of decorative cording)

A variety of buttons and charms

Thread to match (or contrast with) the felt

CONSTRUCTION

1. Copy the pattern at 200%. Use the enlarged pattern to cut two pieces of felt for the stocking.
2. Measure 5" from the top of the stocking front and mark with a straight pin.
3. Hand stitch buttons and charms at random over the front of the stocking, below the pin marking and not too close to the edges. (Be sure your sewing machine's presser foot has room to take a 1/4" seam without bumping into a button.)
4. With the stocking pieces *wrong sides together*, stitch the front and back of the stocking together using a 1/4" seam. Leave the top open.
5. With *right sides together*, stitch a 1/4" seam to join the short ends of the cuff piece. Press seam to one side.

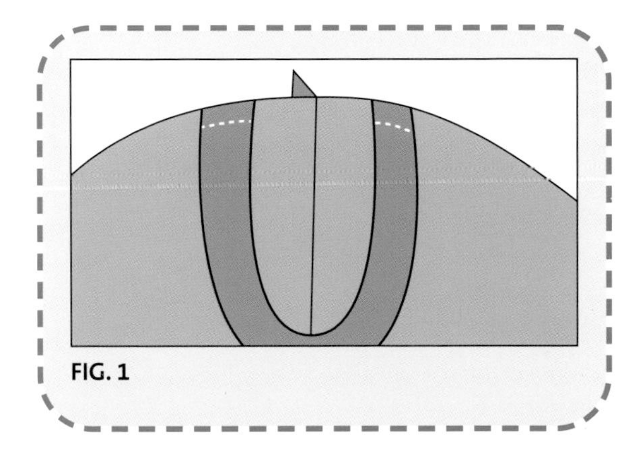

FIG. 1

6. Fold the tab piece in half the long way, *right sides together*, and stitch along the long edge using a 1/4" seam. Trim one side of the seam allowance to 1/8". (Called **grading the seam allowance**, this allows a bulky seam to lie flatter.) Leave the short ends open. Turn the tab right side out (the tab piece now will be 1" x 7"). (Skip this step if you're using cording for the tab.)
7. Pin the tab into place inside the stocking, with one end of the tab on each side of the stocking's left side seam, matching the ends of the tab to the top of the stocking. (Fig. 1)
8. With the *right side out*, slip the cuff inside the stocking. Matching the cuff seam to the left stocking seam, pin the *right side* of the cuff to the *wrong side* of the stocking, with the tab in between the stocking and cuff.

9. Stitch the cuff to the stocking using a $\frac{1}{4}$" seam. Stitch over the tab a second time to secure.

10. Pull the cuff to the outside and turn down just above the stitching line, pulling the tab up, and press the top edges.

TO MAKE YOUR OWN QUILTED CUFF

1. Cut 8 pieces 2" x $6\frac{1}{4}$" from fabrics of your choice.

2. Cut 2 pieces of fabric 2" x $3\frac{1}{4}$" from fabrics of your choice.

3. Join three of the 2" x $6\frac{1}{4}$" pieces together, end to end, using $\frac{1}{4}$" seams. (Fig. 2, Strip A) Repeat, to end up with two A strips.

4. Join the two remaining 2" x $6\frac{1}{4}$" pieces end to end, as above. Add one 2" x $3\frac{1}{4}$" piece to each end. This is the B strip. (Fig. 3, Strip B)

5. Join one Strip A to Strip B along the long edges. Add the other Strip A on the opposite side of Strip B, so Strip B is sandwiched in between the two A strips. (Fig. 4)

6. Trim finished piece to measure $17\frac{1}{2}$" long.

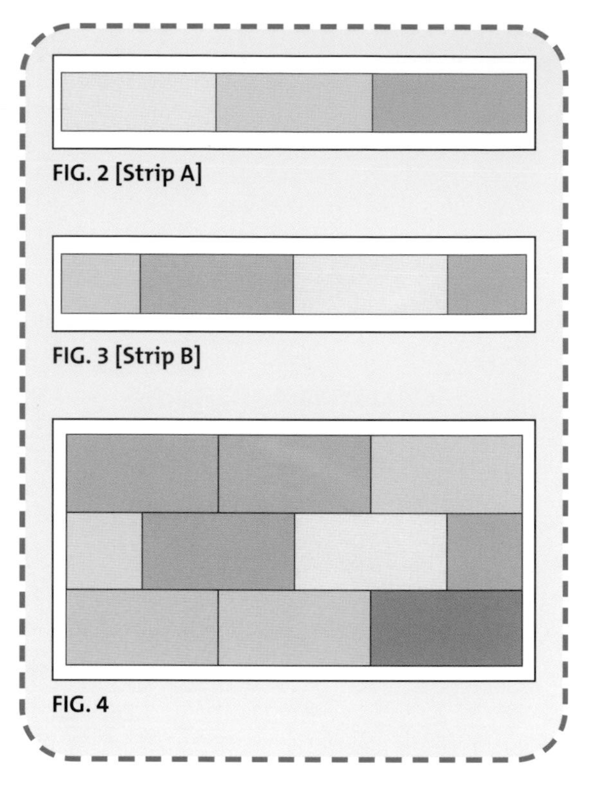

FIG. 2 [Strip A]

FIG. 3 [Strip B]

FIG. 4

7. Cut one piece of batting and one piece of backing fabric, each 6" x 18" long.

8. Layer the backing (wrong side up), the batting, and the pieced strip (right side up), and quilt by stitching through all three layers along the seam lines of the A-B-A strips. (This is called **stitching in the ditch**.)

9. Trim backing and batting to match the top ($5\frac{1}{2}$" x $17\frac{1}{2}$").

10. Bind one long edge using purchased $\frac{1}{2}$"-wide bias tape, or make a binding using the directions in First-Rate Bindings on page 15.

11. Sew the short ends of the mini-quilt together, using a $\frac{1}{4}$" seam.

12. Complete stocking as outlined on pages 65–66.

free-form fun pillow

Loosen up creativity-wise as you doodle free-form style with fabric strips on the front of this cute pillow. It can be finished in under an hour!

Difficulty:

DESIGNER

Ann Brouillette

FINISHED SIZE

14" x 14"

MATERIALS

1/2 yd. pink-and-white check

2 fat quarters (18" x 22") of coordinating plaids

14" pillow form

CUTTING

From the checked fabric:

- 1 square 14 1/2" x 14 1/2"
- 2 strips 9" x 14 1/2"

From one fat quarter:

- Several 3/8"-wide bias strips

From second fat quarter:

- Several 1/2"-wide bias strips

quilt wise

To cut bias strips, first cut the fat quarter to 18" square. Then cut the square in half on the diagonal. Cut strips using the long diagonal edge as the starting point. Be careful not to stretch the bias edges.

CONSTRUCTION

1. To design your pillow top, lay a 1/2"-wide bias strip on top of the 14 1/2" square of checked fabric, curving the strip around until you like the way it looks. Next, lay a 3/8"-wide bias strip right on top of the 1/2"-wide strip, and pin in place. Sew down the middle of the strip set. Repeat this process with additional strip sets until you are satisfied with your design. This is the pillow front.
2. To make the pillow back, turn under 1/4" to the wrong side of one long edge of a 9" x 14 1/2" strip. Then turn under another 1/4", press, and topstitch down. Repeat for the other backing strip.
3. Lay the front of the pillow right side up. Place the backing pieces right side down on the pillow top with the finished edges in the middle, and matching the raw edges of the backing pieces to the pillow front. (The backing pieces will overlap in the center.) Sew 1/4" from the edge all the way around the pillow. Trim corners, and turn right side out.
4. Machine wash and dry the pillow cover once or twice. This will cause the bias strips to fray.
5. Insert the pillow form through the overlapping back flaps.

mini masterpiece

Delight a special youngster in your life by turning their original artwork into a quilted wall hanging. Using a photo transfer, a bit of stitching, and a few beads, you can complete this simple project in an afternoon. The dinosaur in the sample piece was made from a collage created by five-year-old Carli Ann Northrop, the designer's granddaughter.

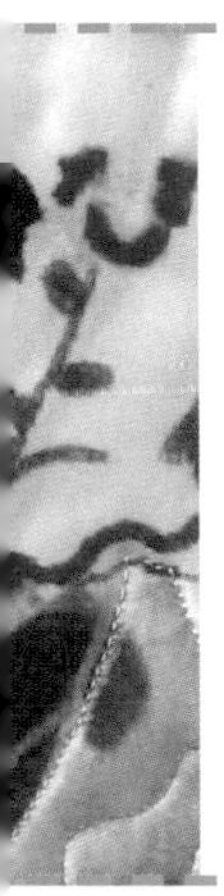

Difficulty:

DESIGNER

Val Deane Osmers

FINISHED SIZE

8½" x 11"

MATERIALS

Child's drawing

Fabrics for photo transfer, backing, and borders as desired

Embellishments as desired

TRANSFERRING PHOTOS TO FABRIC

There are several ways to transfer photos to fabric. Carli's dinosaur collage was scanned using a flat-bed scanner, and then the file was e-mailed directly to a copy shop online. Within hours, an iron-on photo transfer was picked up and was ironed onto a piece of satin using a press. The white border was part of this printing process.

Another method that will give the finished piece a more matte finish is to use a color ink-jet printer to print the image directly onto pretreated fabric. Paper-backed, pretreated fabrics are available in sheets and rolls. You can also create your own printable fabric sheets by treating the fabric with Bubble Jet Set 2000®, ironing the treated fabric to freezer paper, and then running it through an ink-jet printer at high resolution. Both the commercial pretreated fabric sheets and fabric treated with Bubble Jet Set 2000® produce soft, washable images on fabric.

do it right: Quilt artist Caryl Bryer Fallert provides helpful tips for using Bubble Jet Set 2000® on her website, www.bryerpatch.com.

CONSTRUCTION

After transferring the artwork to fabric, layer the photo transfer over a thin batting, and outline stitch around the main images. Cut away the batting just outside the stitching line. This extra layer of batting creates a trapunto effect, adding dimension to the finished piece. If your picture has several images, you may choose to use trapunto under some or all of them, or not at all.

Add beads to the image by trapping them underneath a fine tulle on the surface. In the sample piece, beads were scattered within the designs on the dinosaur's back. (See detail photo.) The tulle was placed over the top of the beads and free-motion-stitched down. You may stitch between and around beads, if desired, or leave them loose within the netting.

If you want borders, now is the time to add them.

Next, cut a piece of batting the size of the entire piece. Place the batting under the piece, and quilt as desired through these two layers. To finish the piece, turn the front edges under on all four sides and press. Cut a piece of backing fabric a scant ½" longer and wider than the top. Turn under all four edges ¼" and press. Then stitch the backing to the turned-under edges of the front by hand or machine.

Add a hanging sleeve (see Be a Show-off on page 17), or display the piece in a frame. Either way, your budding artist will be pleased to see the finished piece on display!

old becomes new

Are you a pack rat? Do you live by your grandma's old adage, "Waste not, want not"? If so, then you've probably collected a good stack of worn-out jeans, and years of T-shirts from high school, college, and concerts. Here are three projects that'll put them back to work. Add some soft flannel and turn those old jeans into a hard-working throw and pillow. The Shoo-Fly Rag Throw is as much at home in the den or dorm room as it is at a picnic or football game. Add the From Scraps to Stitches Pillow for a casual, carefree look in the bedroom. Combine four favorite T-shirts to make Not Your Usual T-shirt Quilt. Multiply the T-shirts to make the quilt as big as you like!

shoo-fly rag throw

What a great way to use up all those soft, weathered jeans that you just hate to throw away! Cut patches from the legs, front, and seat, wherever the fabric hasn't worn through. Add some soft flannel and stitch it all together for a comfortable, heavy-duty throw.

Difficulty:

DESIGNER

Tomme J. Fent

FINISHED SIZE

70" x 70"

FINISHED BLOCK SIZE

10" x 10"

MATERIALS

Approx. 15 pairs of adult jeans in varying shades (If you prefer to buy yardage, 3 3/4 yd. of 60"-wide, or 5 1/4 yd. of 42"-wide denims)

Red-and-black plaid flannel: 5 yd. of 60" wide, or 6 1/2 yd. of 42" wide

mix it up: Want a look that's funkier? Softer? Wilder? It's easy to vary the look; just pick a flannel to suit your taste!

CUTTING

Read through entire pattern before you begin cutting.

From the plaid flannel (cut in this order):

- 50 12" squares
- 4 7½" squares
- 16 6½" squares

From the denim:

- 152 6½" squares
- 4 7½" squares
- 4 12" squares

CONSTRUCTION

- All seams are sewn ***wrong sides together.***
- Use a very small stitch length (1.5 mm) for piecing.
- Backstitch at beginning and end of all seams.
- Clean bobbin case and change sewing machine needle frequently.
- To achieve the look of the sample quilt, vary the shades of blues in adjoining patches throughout the quilt.

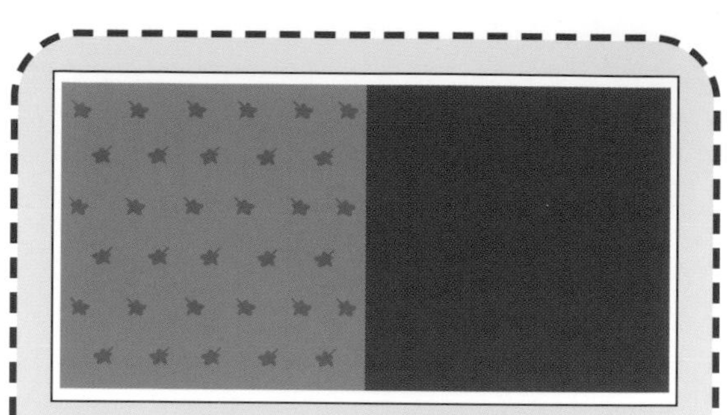

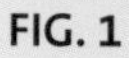

FIG. 1

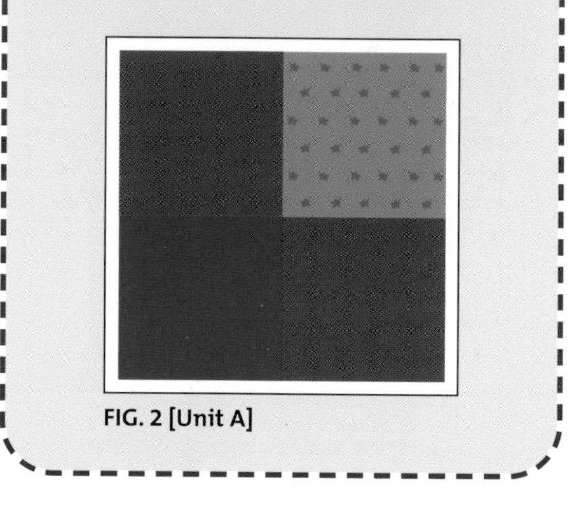

FIG. 2 [Unit A]

MAKING THE FOUR-PATCH BLOCKS

Unit A

1. Join two 6½" denim squares, wrong sides together, *using a ½" seam allowance.* (Fig. 1)
2. Repeat step 1 with two more 6½" denim squares.
3. *Using a ½" seam allowance*, join the two units from steps 1 and 2, wrong sides together, with the seams opposing. (See Opposites Attract on page 10.) This is **Unit A.** (Fig. 2)
4. Repeat steps 1, 2, and 3 another 31 times to make a **total of 32** Unit A patches.

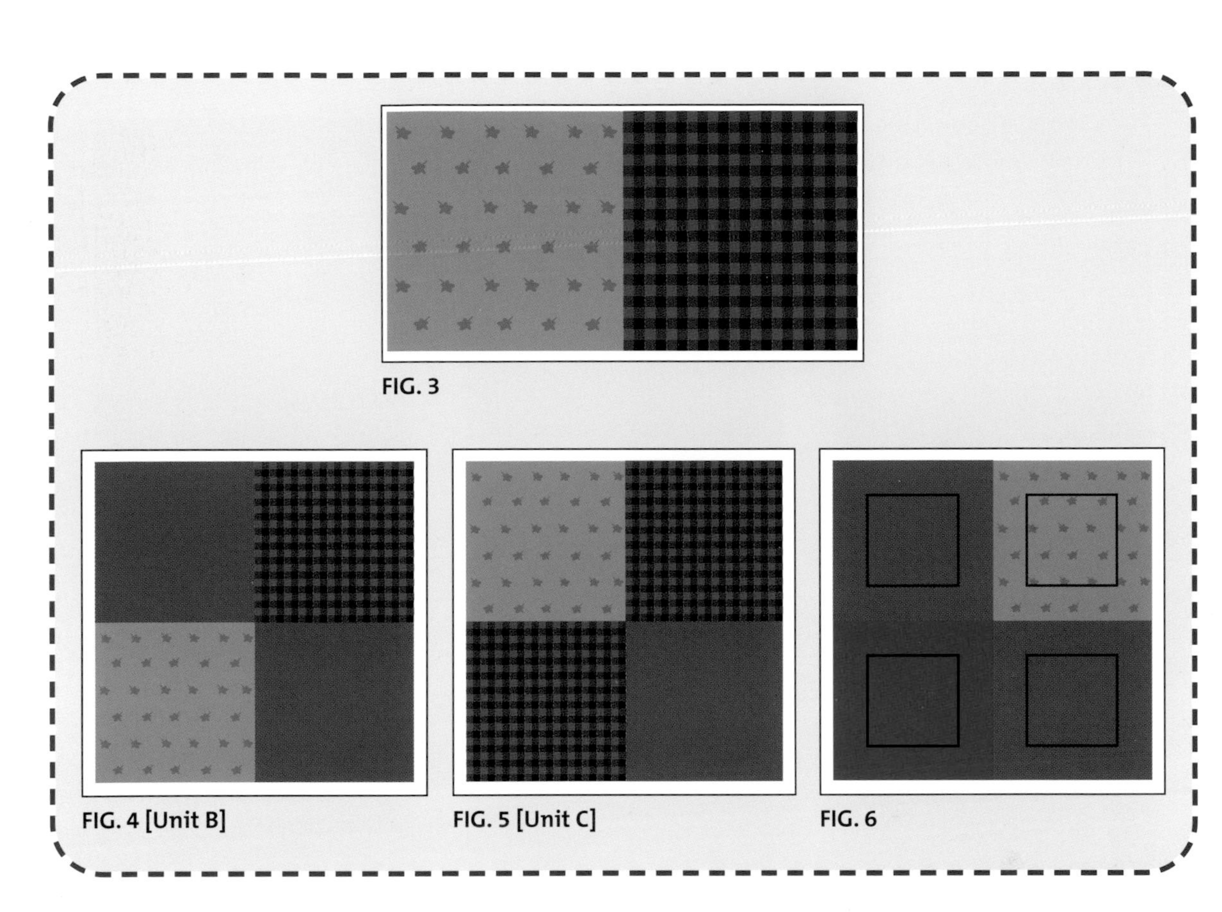
FIG. 3

FIG. 4 [Unit B]

FIG. 5 [Unit C]

FIG. 6

Unit B

5. Repeat step 1. Repeat step 2, but instead of using two 6½" denim squares, use one denim square and one 6½" flannel square. (Fig. 3) Using a ½" seam allowance, join these two units, wrong sides together, with seams opposing. This is **Unit B.** (Fig. 4) Repeat these steps another 3 times for a **total of 4** Unit B patches.

Unit C

6. Repeat step 1, but instead of using two 6½" denim squares, use one denim square and one 6½" flannel square. (Fig. 3) Repeat another 7 times for a **total of 8** of these patches.
7. With the flannel squares on opposite sides, join two of the units you made in step 6, wrong sides together, seams opposing, using a ½" seam allowance. This is **Unit C.** (Fig. 5) Repeat another 3 times for a **total of 4** Unit C patches.
8. Place a completed four-patch unit (Unit A, Unit B, or Unit C) atop a 12" flannel square, wrong sides together. Quilt a 3½" square in each quadrant of the block. (Fig. 6)

do it right: You may choose to quilt a different shape in the quadrants of the four-patch blocks. Just be sure your chosen motif is no larger than 3½" in length or width.

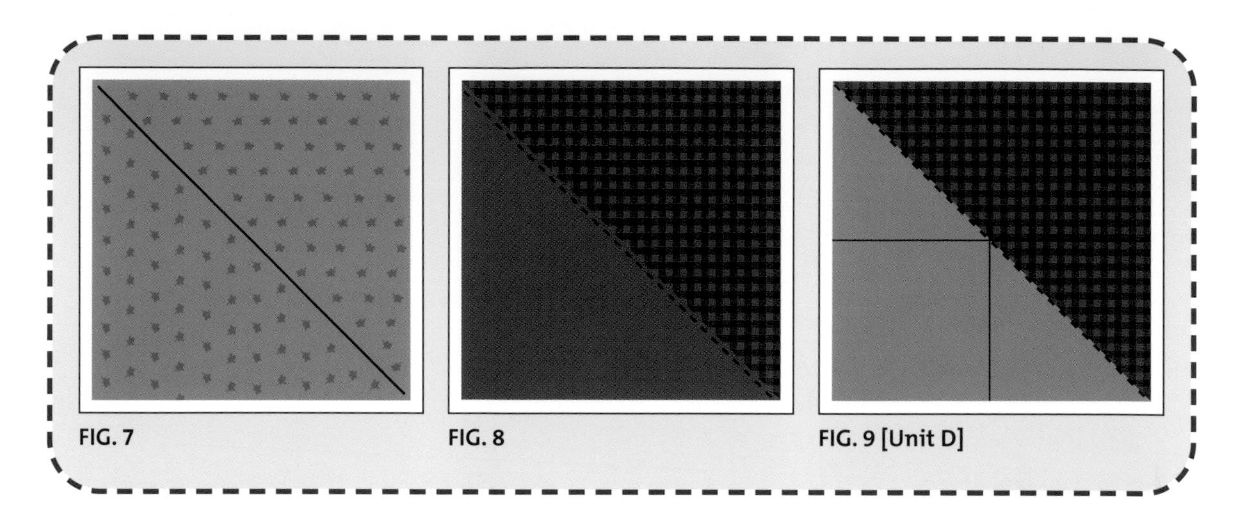
FIG. 7 FIG. 8 FIG. 9 [Unit D]

9. Repeat step 8 another 39 times, using all of the Unit A, Unit B, and Unit C patches, for a **total of 40** four-patch blocks.

MAKING THE HALF-SQUARE TRIANGLE FOUR-PATCH BLOCKS (UNIT D)

Half-Square Triangles

Refer to Triangles Are Square? on page 12, but note that in this project, your fabrics will be *wrong* sides together instead of right sides together.

1. Draw a diagonal line between opposite corners on the *front* of the four 7½" denim squares. (Fig. 7)
2. Place a 7½" denim square atop a 7½" flannel square, wrong sides together, with the denim square facing up. Stitch a scant ¼" on each side of the drawn line.
3. Cut on the drawn line and unfold at the diagonal seams, making two half-square triangles. (Fig. 8)
4. Square up the block to 6½" square, making sure the triangles are equal in size. (The diagonal line should still run from corner to corner when you finish squaring up the block.)
5. Repeat steps 1–4 another 7 times for a **total of 8** half-square triangle patches.

Unit D

6. Make 4 four-patch blocks using 2 half-square triangle patches (from step 5), one 6½" flannel square, and one 6½" denim square. The flannel triangles should always be next to the flannel square. (Fig. 9) This is **Unit D**.

7. Place a completed Unit D block atop a 12" flannel square, wrong sides together. Quilt a 3½" square in the square quadrants of the block. Quilt close to each side of the diagonal line in the center of the half-square triangle patches (without catching the seam allowance as you quilt). (Fig. 10) Repeat another 3 times for a **total of 4** half-square triangle four-patch blocks.

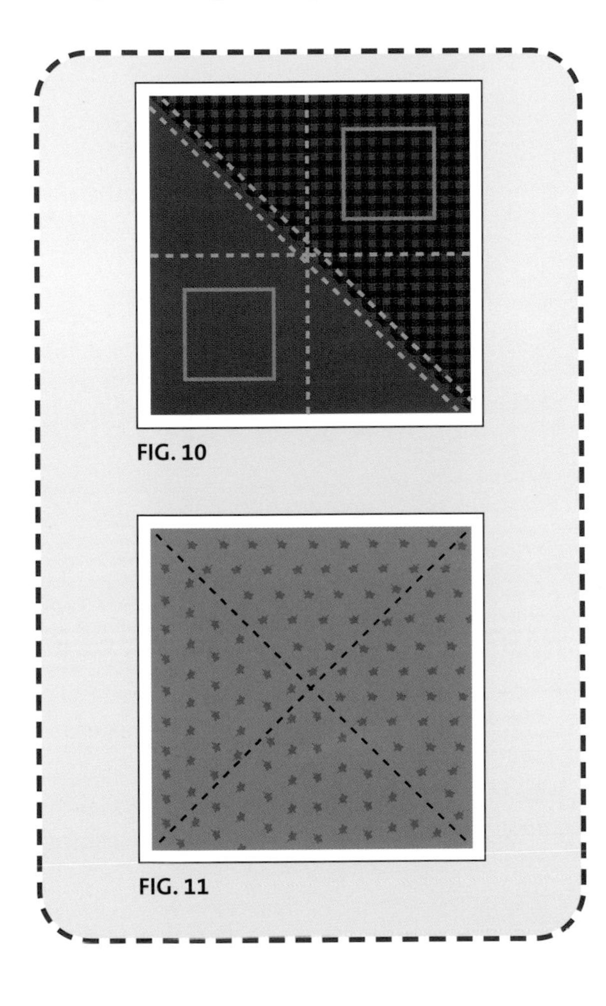

FIG. 10

FIG. 11

X SQUARES

1. Place a 12" denim square atop a 12" flannel square, wrong sides together. Quilt diagonal lines from corner to corner to form an X in the middle of the square. (Fig. 11) Repeat another 3 times for a **total of 4** denim-and-flannel X-square patches.
2. Place two 12" flannel squares together and quilt an X as in step 1, for a **total of 1** flannel X-square block.

quilt wise

Rag throws like this one can be made from any loosely woven fabrics. For a lighter-weight throw, try plaid homespuns. No batting is required.

PUTTING IT ALL TOGETHER

Now you're ready to join the blocks into rows, and join the rows to make the quilt. *All the blocks and rows will be joined using a 1" seam allowance.*

1. Lay out all the blocks, with the Shoo-Fly block in the center, as shown in Fig. 12. Check to be sure the flannel blocks are oriented correctly in the corners and in the Shoo-Fly block. Play with the arrangement until you're satisfied with the placement of light and dark denims throughout the quilt.
2. Join the blocks in horizontal rows, wrong sides together, seams opposing, *using a 1" seam allowance.* Then join the rows, wrong sides together, seams opposing, again using a 1" seam allowance.

   do it right: Recheck the placement of the flannel patches before stitching; the tiny stitch length makes it difficult to remove stitches!

3. When all rows are joined together, stitch 1" from the outside edge all the way around the quilt.

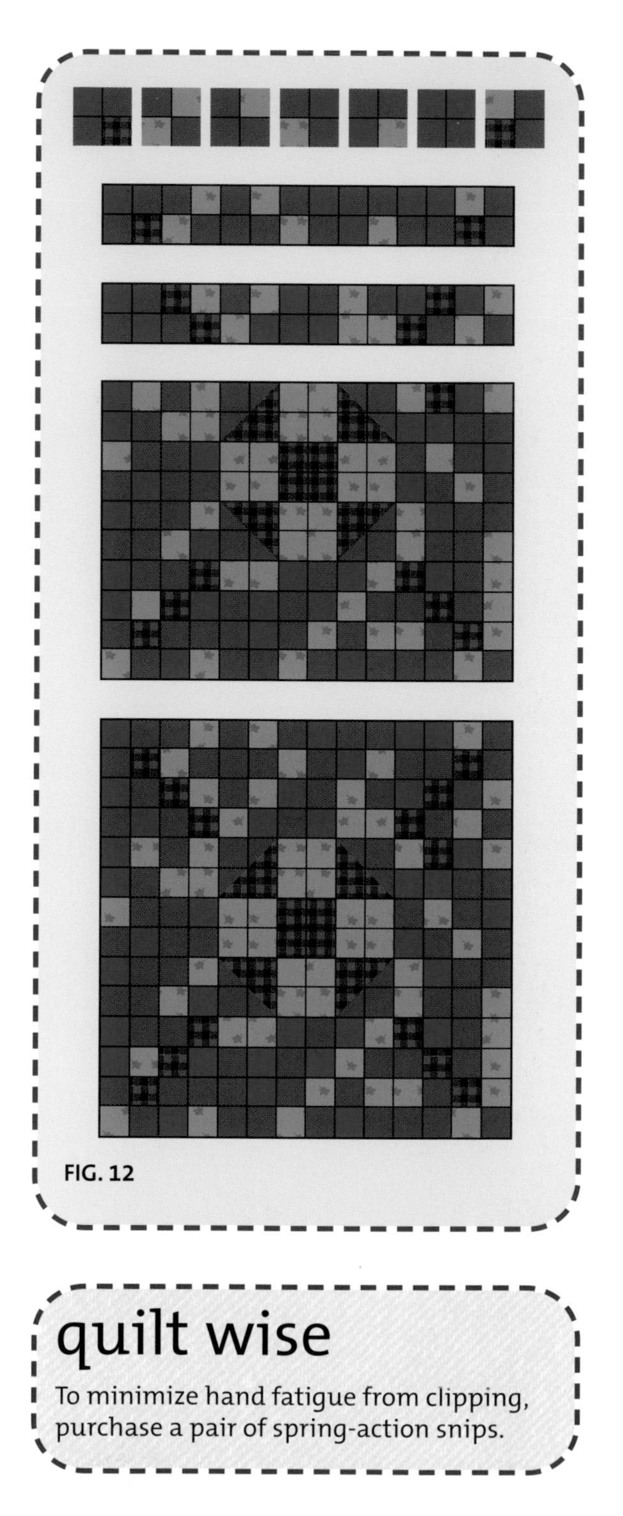

FIG. 12

CLIPPING THE SEAMS—THE MESSY PART!

Clip every seam in the entire quilt. Clips in the 1" seams should be 1" to 1½" apart. Clips in the ½" seams, and in the ¼" seams in the half-square triangles, should be about ½" apart. Stop your clips a few threads from the seam allowance: *do not clip into or through the stitching.* Remember to clip all around the outside edge of the quilt, stopping a few threads from the stitching line.

quilt wise

To minimize hand fatigue from clipping, purchase a pair of spring-action snips.

LET'S GET RAGGY

The finishing touches are washing the quilt and drying it in the dryer to fray the seams.

tips for washing and drying

- Unless you want to become really good friends with your plumber, it's a good idea to take your finished throw to a commercial laundry to wash and dry for the first time. The large quantity of threads from the ragged edges can clog your pipes!
- Use a washing machine designed for oversize loads. This throw is very heavy!
- When you dry the throw, add one or two *dry* towels to help the quilt dry faster. (This works for any quilt.) You can also wash a couple of pairs of jeans or a tennis shoe with the throw, and then put these in the dryer with the throw to help fray the seams. If more fraying is desired, repeat washing and drying, or brush the seam allowances with a stiff brush.

from scraps to stitches pillow

Patches of soft, weathered jeans go from warming your legs to cushioning your head in this overstuffed pillow, backed with soft flannel.

Difficulty:

DESIGNER

Tomme J. Fent

FINISHED SIZE

20" x 20"

MATERIALS

2 to 3 pairs of old jeans, cut up into 16 squares 6½" x 6½"

22" square of flannel in your choice of color and pattern (sample uses blue-and-black plaid)

2 bags (20 oz.) of polyester fiberfill

CONSTRUCTION

Refer to Figs. 1 and 2 in the Shoo-Fly Rag Throw pattern to make these blocks. Use a short stitch length (2 mm) for all piecing.

1. Join two 6½" denim squares, *wrong sides together*, using a ½" seam allowance. Repeat 7 more times, for a total of 8 of these units.
2. Using a ½" seam allowance, join 2 of the units from step 1, *wrong sides together*, with the seams opposing. (See Opposites Attract on page 10.) Repeat 3 more times for a total of 4 of these four-patch blocks.
3. Join 2 of the four-patch blocks, *wrong sides together*, this time using a 1" seam allowance. Repeat with the other 2 blocks.
4. Join the 2 sets of four-patch blocks, *wrong sides together*, using a 1" seam allowance, to make 1 large block 22"x 22".
5. Clip all of the ½" seams about every ½", *taking care not to clip into or through the stitching*. Clip the 1" seams about every inch.
6. With *wrong sides together*, sew the jeans block to the flannel square, using a 1" seam allowance. Leave an opening in the center of one side that is large enough to get your fist through.
7. Stuff the pillow. Use small handfuls of fiberfill at a time, and pull the fiberfill apart to fluff before stuffing into pillow. Don't compact the fiberfill too tightly into the pillow or the pillow won't be soft. Remember to poke fiberfill into each of the corners.
8. After stuffing, close the opening, maintaining the 1" seam allowance.
9. Clip around the outside edge of the pillow, again *taking care not to clip into or through the stitching*.
10. Wash the pillow in mild detergent and dry it in the dryer to fray the seams. When drying, add a pair or two of *dry* jeans to speed drying and help fray the pillow's seams. If more fraying is desired, repeat washing and drying, or brush the seam allowances with a stiff brush.

not your usual t-shirt quilt

T-shirts are something we all have plenty of. Select four of your favorites and whip up this distinctive wall hanging as a lasting reminder of good times and good friends. Unlike many T-shirt quilts that are made up of large, repetitious blocks cut from the T-shirts, this quirky quilt intersperses black sashing to create a peekaboo effect. The pattern is for a wall hanging using four T-shirts, but you can enlarge it easily to any size simply by using more T-shirts.

Difficulty:

DESIGNER

Jane Vereen

FINISHED SIZE

38" x 37"

MATERIALS

4 brightly colored T-shirts with interesting logos

1½ yd. fusible knit interfacing (22" wide), less if interfacing is wider

1 yd. black textured fabric for sashing and inner border

1¼ yd. black-and-white polka dot fabric for outer borders (This is the yardage needed without piecing the borders. If borders are pieced, you will need ½ yard.)

1¼ yd. backing fabric

⅓ yd. black-and-brights print for binding

CUTTING

- From each of the T-shirts, cut out the main logo centered in a 12½" square.
- From the fusible interfacing, cut four 12½" squares.
- From the black textured fabric, cut 10 strips 1½" x 12" and 1 strip 1½" x 26", for sashing. Also cut 2 strips 2½" x 26", and 2 strips 2½" x 29" for inner borders.
- From the black-and-white polka dot fabric, cut 2 strips 4½" x 29" and 2 strips 4½" x 37" for outer borders.
- From the black-and-brights print, cut 4 strips 2⅛" wide for binding.

CONSTRUCTION

1. Fuse interfacing to the back of each of the T-shirt logos, following the manufacturer's instructions. After fusing, trim each shirt to 12" square.
2. With the logo in a vertical position, cut each shirt into 3 columns, 4" wide each.

quilt wise

Instead of adding a traditional binding, you can also make your backing 3" larger than the quilt top for a **self-binding**. Center the quilt on the backing, and quilt as desired. Trim the backing to a consistent width on all sides of the quilt. On each of the two sides, fold the backing in to meet the edge of the quilt and press. Repeat on the top and bottom of the quilt. Then fold the sides in again, bringing the backing over the edge to the front of the quilt, and stitch in place by hand or machine, using matching thread. Repeat on the top and bottom. This should create nice, square corners on your quilt.

3. Stitch 1 of the 1½" x 12" strips of black textured fabric between each of the columns, creating a 5-piece block.
4. Join 2 of the blocks, side by side, using 1 of the 1½" x 12" strips of black textured fabric. Repeat with the remaining 2 blocks and 1½" x 12" strip.
5. Join the 2 rows of blocks as shown in the photo, using the 1½" x 26" strip of black

textured fabric. You have now completed the center of your quilt!

6. Add the two $2\frac{1}{2}$" x 26" strips to the top and bottom of the quilt center. Then add the two $2\frac{1}{2}$" x 29" strips to the sides.
7. Add the two $4\frac{1}{2}$" x 29" strips of black-and-white polka dotted fabric to the top and bottom of the quilt. Then add the two $4\frac{1}{2}$" x 37" strips to the sides.
8. Layer with batting and back, and quilt as desired.
9. Bind according to the instructions in First-Rate Bindings, on page 15, or create a self-binding as described in the "quilt wise" tip box on page 85.
10. Add a label and a hanging sleeve if desired. See Be a Show-off (page 17) and Make It Personal (page 19).

all tied up

Vintage neckties are all the rage, turning up in clothing and accessories in all sorts of unexpected ways. They're available in a wealth of colors and patterns, from preppy to funky, and you can find them everywhere, from thrift shops to your relatives' closets. (Just be sure to get permission; you don't want to cut up your dad's favorite tie!) In this chapter we present three projects that make playful use of vintage ties: two different styles of halter tops and an ultra-cool bag with beaded fringe. First let's talk about preparing ties for quilting. Our thanks to designers Sophia Snider and Zelma Abbott for the following tips on working with ties. Turn the page. . . .

get ready to quilt: preparing the ties

Vintage neckties are made from a variety of fabrics, including silk, rayon, cotton, wool, and polyester. Sometimes you won't know the fabric content, and often you won't know who wore the tie before it landed in your hands. Therefore, always wash ties before using them in a project. They should be hand washed in a mild soap, such as Mountain Mist® Ensure or Orvus® Paste Quilt Soap, available through your local quilt shop. Rinse until the water runs clear. You may have to wash and rinse several times. If a tie continues to bleed, discard it: you don't want your hard work to be ruined by running colors.

When they're clean, remove the ties from the water, lay them out lengthwise on a towel, and roll up the towel. Squeeze out the excess water: You can sit on the rolled-up towel, or have a friend hold tightly to one end of the towel while you hold the other end and twist. Unroll the towel and hang the ties up to dry. (Hanging them on hangers around the house may start some interesting conversations.)

When the ties are dry, carefully pick apart the center seam, being careful not to cut or stretch the fabric. Open the center seam and remove the interfacing or webbing. Leave the lining fabric in place as a stabilizer, or you may remove it if desired. Press the ties flat with your iron set at its lowest temperature, as some tie fabrics will melt or scorch even at moderate temperatures. Test the iron temperature on a small patch at the narrow end of the tie, and use a pressing cloth, if necessary. Also, be careful while pressing because ties are cut on the bias and can stretch out of shape easily.

Now you're ready to use the ties in your quilting projects. For clothing, it's a good idea to use ties with similar fabric content. To calculate how many ties you'll need for a project, keep in mind that most ties will be about twice as wide after they are taken apart. The wider the ties, the fewer you will need.

tie-one-on halter top

Join the retro craze when you wear this '70s-inspired halter top made from vintage neckties.

DESIGNER

Sophia Snider

MATERIALS

2 extra-wide ties or 3 to 4 narrower ties (the wider, the better)

$1\frac{1}{2}$ yd. lightweight fusible interfacing

$1\frac{1}{2}$ yd. of 100% cotton print for lining, in colors to coordinate with ties

Thread in neutral color for piecing (Dark gray is good for darker ties; taupe and beige are good for lighter ties.)

Embroidery floss in colors to match, or contrast with, the ties

Embroidery needle

Tailor's chalk or temporary fabric marker (see Marking Tools on page 7)

Tape measure

CONSTRUCTION

Read through all the instructions before you begin to cut and sew.

MAKING THE BRA AND NECKTIE PIECES

1. Prepare ties as described in the introduction to this section. If you are using extra-wide ties, round the point on the wide end, cutting off as little fabric as possible. (Fig. 1) The two ties will be used as the bra portion of the top and the neck ties (no pun intended!).

   If you are using narrower ties, you can piece them together to make them wide enough. Pick a tie for the center color of one bra section. Take another tie and cut it lengthwise down the middle. (Fig. 2) Sew one-half to each side of the center tie, so the V at the center bottom continues up each side. (Fig. 3) Press the seams open. Pick a tie for the center color of the other bra section, and repeat.

2. Make sure both bra pieces are the same size, and check to see that they will fit you. Trim or add fabric as needed.

3. Using the bra pieces as a guide, cut interfacing and fuse to the wrong sides of both bra pieces, following the manufacturer's directions, but using the same heat setting you used for the ties. (It may take a bit longer to fuse than with a hotter iron, but you won't risk ruining your top.)

4. Pin the bra pieces right side up on the *wrong* side of a single layer of the lining fabric. Cut lining for each of the bra pieces.

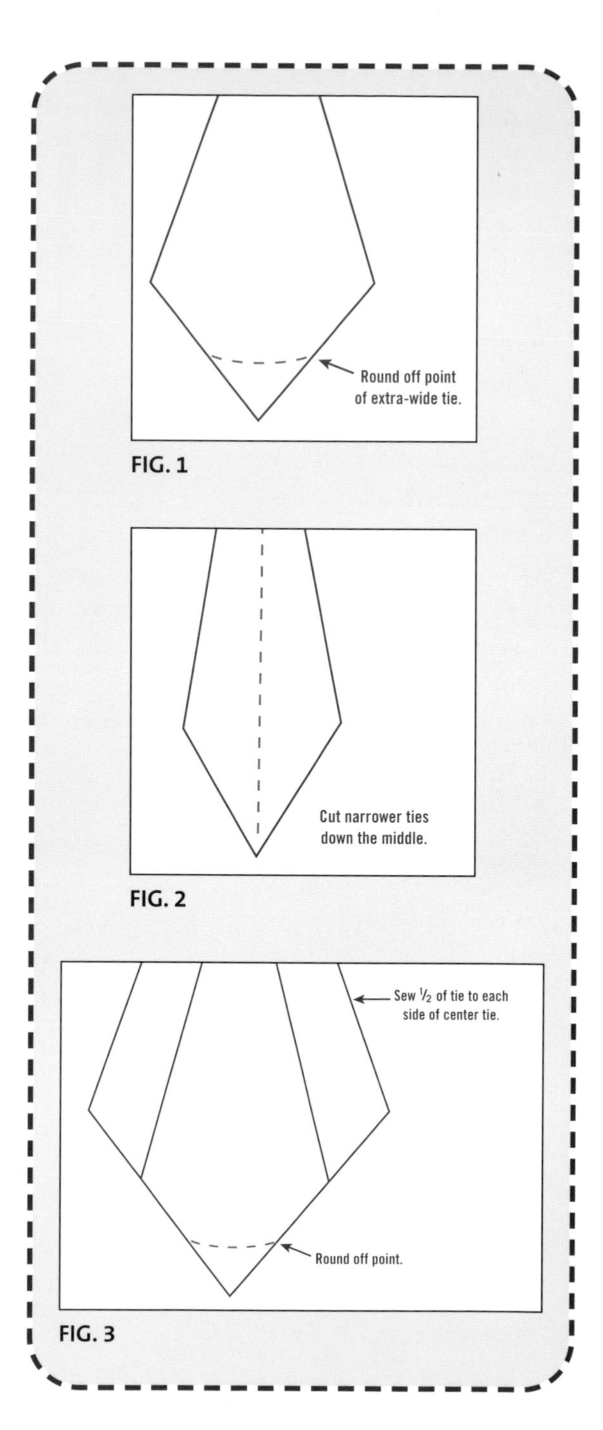

FIG. 1
FIG. 2
FIG. 3

5. Place bra pieces and lining pieces right sides together. Stitch around the sides and top with a 3/8" seam allowance, leaving the rounded edge at the bottom unstitched. Clip corners, turn right side out, and press.

6. Gather the lower, rounded edge of the bra pieces, as follows. Stitch with a long basting stitch 1/4" from raw edge, and again 3/8" from raw edge. Leave the thread tails long on both ends of the stitching lines. Mark the center of the bra piece. From each side, pull the bobbin threads and scoot the fabric in toward the center until the fabric is gathered enough to form a cup that will fit you (or the person you're making the top for). Make sure that the gathers are even and that both cups are gathered the same amount. Tie off the thread tails so you won't lose any of the gathers as you complete the top.

MAKING THE BAND

1. Select one tie for the band the bra sections will be sewn onto (the piece that goes from side to side, under the breasts). You will use the narrow portion of a tie for the band. If the tie is too short, take the narrow portions of two ties, cut the ends off straight, join the ties, and place the seam at the center front of the band. When you have a piece long enough to go from one side to the other under your breasts, use your rotary cutter to straighten one long side of the strip. Using this straight edge as a guide, cut a strip 3 1/2" wide. You will be cutting on the bias, so take care not to stretch the fabric. Square off the ends.

2. Cut a 3 1/2" strip of interfacing the same length as your band, and fuse to the wrong side of the band, following the manufacturer's instructions but using the same heat setting you used for the ties.

3. From the lining fabric, cut 2 strips 6" x 22", and 1 strip 3 1/2" wide and the length of your band. Set aside the 3 1/2" strip for later. Fold the 6" x 22" strips in half lengthwise, right sides together (so they are now 3" x 22"). Stitch down the long edge and across one end using a 1/2" seam allowance. Clip corners, and turn the tube right side out. Press. Pin one of the tubes on the front side of the band, matching the raw edges of the tube to one end of the band. (Fig. 4) Measure 1/2" from each side of the short end and mark. Stitch the tube to the band *between the marks* with a 1/2" seam allowance, leaving 1/2" free at the beginning and end of the seam. Place the other tube on the other end of the band and repeat as directed. Don't press the seam at this point; leave the tubes lying across the front of the band.

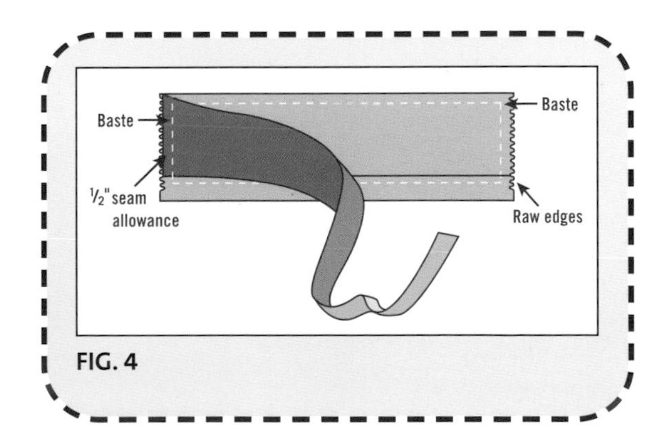

FIG. 4

PUTTING IT ALL TOGETHER

1. Pin the right sides of the bra sections to the right side of the band. Begin by placing one edge of each cup in the center of the band. Adjust the cup placement as needed to fit the wearer, spacing the cups apart as needed or desired. Baste using a 3/8" seam allowance, and recheck the fit. Then stitch using a 1/2" seam allowance.
2. Pin the band lining (the 3 1/2" strip you set aside earlier) to the band, right sides together, matching raw edges. (The tubes you stitched to the band earlier will be between the band and the band lining.) Stitch using a 1/2" seam allowance, beginning with a backstitch at the outer edge of one bra cup, and then proceeding across to the side, down the side, across the bottom, up the other side, and across to the outer edge of the other bra cup, ending with another backstitch. Be sure not to catch any portion of the tubes in the seam allowance. Turn right side out and press.
3. Press under 1/2" on the top of the band lining. Slip stitch the lining in place on the back side of the band.
4. Using a chalk pencil or fabric marker (see Marking Tools on page 7), draw simple flowers or other designs of your choice on the bra cups.

   do it right: As you position your flower designs, keep in mind where the design will fall on the wearer's body!

   To use the flower design as shown on the sample top, trace the pattern and cut out around the outside edge. Lay the pattern on the top, and draw around the petals using the chalk pencil or fabric marker. Remove the pattern and draw the center circle.
5. Quilt by stitching around your designs with a running stitch, using three strands of embroidery floss. Choose a floss color similar to the halter top for a subtle effect, or contrasting floss colors for more noticeable designs.

   Your Tie-One-On halter top is now ready to wear! To keep the top looking new, remember to wash it gently, using the same soap you used to wash the ties, and hang to dry. Press as needed with a cool iron.

fit-to-be-tied halter top

Tie this cute top on your own flower child for some retro fun!

Difficulty:

DESIGNER

Sophia Snider

MATERIALS

3 to 5 ties, depending on width (top in photo used three ties)

1/2 yd. lightweight fusible interfacing

1/4 to 1/2 yd. of 100% coordinating cotton fabric for lining (amount needed depends on size you're making)

Thread in neutral color for piecing (dark gray is good for darker ties; taupe and beige are good for lighter ties)

2 yd. soft 1/2" cording for ties

Embroidery floss in colors to match or contrast with the ties

Embroidery needle

Tailor's chalk or temporary fabric marker (see Marking Tools on page 7)

Tape measure

CONSTRUCTION

Refer to the drawing as you go through these steps.

1. Prepare ties as described in the introduction to this section.
2. Measure under the wearer's breasts from side to side, and add 2" to this measurement. Make a note of the total. You will build your tie fabric to this width at the widest point.
3. Decide on the order in which you want the ties to appear. Using a 3/8" seam allowance, sew the sides of the ties together matching the widest points, with all the wide ends facing down. (Fig. 1) Stitch together enough ties to make the widest area as big as the measurement you figured in step 1. Press seams open.
4. Place the tie unit on your rotary mat and cut a straight edge across the widest part of the unit, as shown in Fig. 1. (To use scissors, mark a cutting line with a ruler across the widest part of the unit and then cut.)
5. Measure from the wearer's collarbone down to the point below the breast line where you want the top to end. Add 4 inches to this measurement for seams and casings. (If the wearer has large breasts, add to this measurement to compensate.)
6. From the straight edge of the tie unit that you cut in step 4, measure the total inches you figured in step 5, and cut the fabric parallel to the first straight edge.
7. Using the tie unit from step 6 as a pattern, cut interfacing to fit, and fuse to the back of the tie unit following the manufacturer's

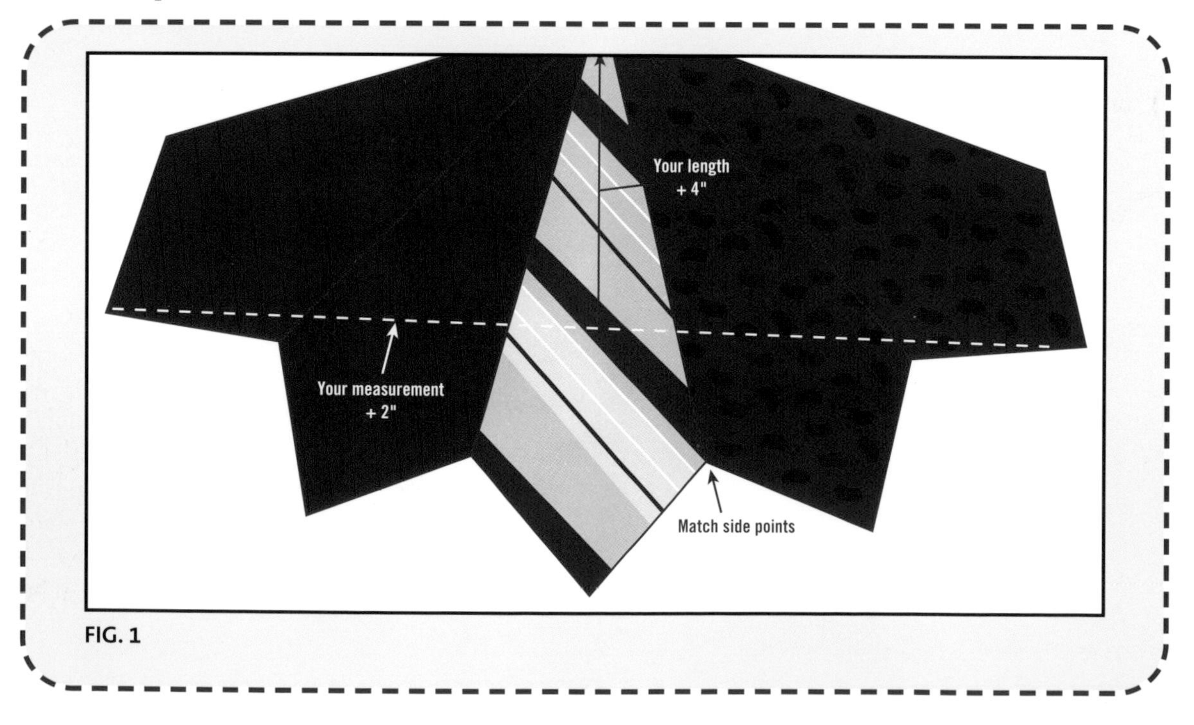

FIG. 1

instructions but using the same iron temperature you used for the ties. (It may take a bit longer to fuse than with a hotter iron, but you won't risk ruining your top.)

8. Pin tie unit onto lining fabric, right sides together, and cut lining to match the tie unit. Stitch tie unit to lining on all sides, right sides together, using a $^3/_8$" seam allowance, and leaving a 3" to 4" opening on one side for turning. Clip corners and turn right side out. Hand stitch the opening closed and press.
9. Fold under 1" on the top and bottom edges of the halter top and stitch in place, easing in any excess fullness on the bottom edge.
10. Measure around the wearer's chest area (all the way around) below the breast line. Add 20" and cut cording to this length. Tie a knot on each end, and thread the cording through the lower casing. Tie a knot on each end of the remaining cording and thread through the top casing.
11. Using the chalk pencil or fabric marker, draw a simple flower or other design of your choice on the center section of the top. To use the flower design as shown on the sample top, trace the pattern and cut out around the outside edge. Lay the pattern on the top and draw around the petals using a chalk pencil or fabric marker. Remove the pattern and draw the center circle.
12. Quilt by stitching around your design with a running stitch, using three strands of embroidery floss. Choose a floss color similar to the halter top for a subtle effect, or contrasting floss colors for more noticeable designs.

The Fit-to-Be-Tied Halter Top is complete! To keep it looking new, remember to wash it gently, using the same soap you used to wash the ties, and hang to dry. Press as needed with a cool iron.

two-way-tie purse

This attention-grabbing purse is too delightful for words! Two extra-wide ties, beaded fringe, and a purchased appliqué come together in a one-of-a-kind purse that's as comfortable with evening wear as it is with jeans. (See page 123 for back view.) Whether the ties are dressy or bold, soft or wild, you'll have fun choosing ties that reflect your personality. Wouldn't an Elvis or Beatles tie make a great purse? How about those vintage geometric ties from the 1950s? Don't be tied down by our ideas; create a purse that's as unique as you are!

Difficulty:

DESIGNER

Zelma Abbott

FINISHED SIZE

Approx. 6" x 9", depending on size of ties

MATERIALS

2 extra-wide neckties

½ yd. lining fabric

1 yd. lightweight fusible interfacing

1 yd. each of 2 different bead-by-the-yard trims to coordinate with the two ties

1 yd. satin cording

1 iron-on appliqué of your choice (sample uses a rose appliqué)

6" zipper in color coordinating with ties

CONSTRUCTION

1. Prepare ties as described in the introduction to this section. Place tie on cutting board with side points lined up along the same line of the board. (Fig. 1) Measure 10½" up the tie from the point and cut straight across. (To cut without a cutting board, mark a straight line on the wrong side of the tie from side point to side point, using tailor's chalk or masking tape. When cutting tie at 10½" point, be sure cut is parallel to the marked line.) Press tie flat. Repeat with second tie. Trim as necessary to make ties the same size and shape.
2. Using one tie as a pattern, cut two pieces of lining fabric and two pieces of fusible interfacing to same size as ties. Fuse interfacing to wrong side of each piece of lining fabric, following manufacturer's instructions.
3. Carefully unstring the first 3 dangles on the string of beaded fringe. Secure the loose thread to the backside of the trim's ribbon. You now will have about ¾" of the ribbon that is unbeaded. Fold the unbeaded portion of the ribbon to the wrong side and take a stitch or two on each edge to hold it in place. Pin beaded fringe to coordinating tie, beginning and ending 1" below the upper raw edge (the edge you cut in step 1).

do it right: Some beaded fringe is attached to pretty ribbon or trim that you will want to show, while other beaded fringe is attached to twill tape or fabric you will want to hide. If you want the ribbon to show, pin so the beaded edge of the trim is ½" from the outside of the tie, and the fringe faces the *outside* of the tie. (The nonbeaded edge falls outside the ½" seam allowance.) (Fig. 2) If you do not want the ribbon to show, pin so the beaded edge of the trim is ½" from the outside of the tie, and the fringe faces the *inside* of the tie. (The nonbeaded edge falls *inside* the seam allowance, and will be hidden when the seam allowance is turned under.) (Fig. 3)

4. Stitch trim in place using a straight stitch, pivoting at corners. Be careful not to let your needle hit a bead.

do it right: For safety, wear eye protection when machine stitching with beads.

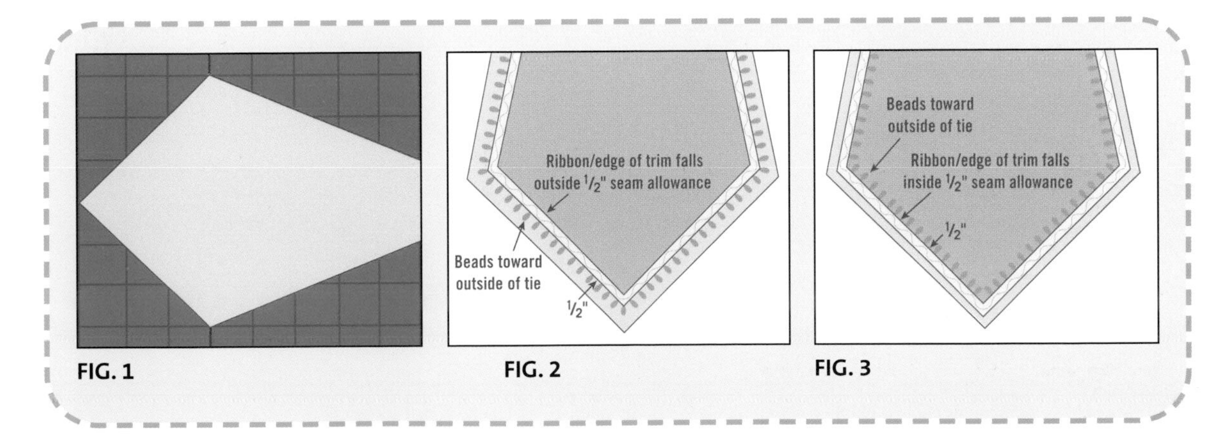

FIG. 1 FIG. 2 FIG. 3

Sew both edges of the trim to the tie.

do it right: If your machine has an oval hole in the throat plate, you can use a double needle and only have to stitch once.

5. Repeat steps 2 and 3 for the other set of trim and the other tie.
6. Center and fuse the appliqué to one tie face.
7. Fold under 1" on upper raw edge of each tie and press lightly. Fold under 1/2" around other edges of tie and press lightly.
8. Center the upper edge of one tie, right side up, on zipper tape and topstitch in place. Repeat to topstitch other tie to other side of zipper tape. (Fig. 4)
9. Pin pressed edges of ties to each other with wrong sides together, matching side points. Whipstitch the two ties together by hand, using matching or neutral thread.

do it right: To keep from catching beaded fringe in the thread as you stitch, fold each side's beads in toward the center of that side and use painter's masking tape (which has lighter adhesive than regular masking tape) to hold the beads out of the way during stitching.

10. To make lining, place lining pieces right sides together. Sew around edges using a 1/2" seam allowance, starting and stopping 1" from top edge, and leaving top edge open. *Do not turn right side out.* Fold top edge of lining down 1" toward wrong side and press.
11. Open zipper and slip lining down inside purse, matching side seams of lining to side seams of purse. Slip stitch the upper folded edge of the lining to the wrong side of the zipper tape just below the row of topstitching that attached the ties to the zipper tape.
12. Tie a knot about 1 1/2" from each end of the satin cording. Carefully unwind, brush out, and fluff the 1 1/2" ends. Lay each end in between the two rows of beaded fringe, with the end about 1" down from the top edge. Whipstitch cording in place using doubled thread.

Enjoy your kicky, unique purse!

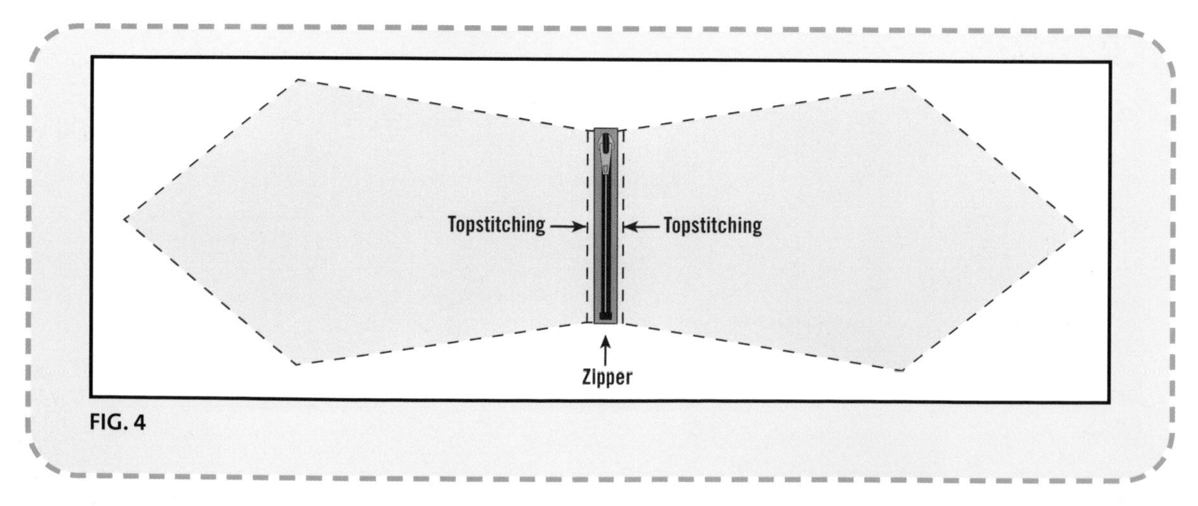

FIG. 4

spectacular spaces

Quilts don't just cover beds anymore; they can be used to decorate throughout the house and lend a personal touch to an office too. There's nothing quite as inviting as a dinner table set with colorful linens that complement the tableware and food. The tasteful Dinner Is Served Table Runner and Placemats will create just the right ambience to greet your guests. Add some candles, put on some jazz, and watch your party come to life! Hang the Amazed Wall Hanging in your living room or office for an attention-grabbing work of art. Redecorating your bedroom is easy when you use the Indigo Nights Quilt as the centerpiece. Its simple, elegant lines help create a haven where you can relax and gather your thoughts. Pair it with the Mum's the Word Wall Hanging for the beginnings of an Asian-inspired bedroom.

dinner is served

table runner and placemats

If your walls are covered with paintings, prints, and photographs, and your shelves are bulging with pottery, turned wood, and glass treasures, this artistic table runner with coordinating placemats will fit right in. Greet your guests with a little Prairie Style and a lot of class when you set your table with this striking contemporary design.

Difficulty:

the table runner

DESIGNER

Tomme J. Fent

FINISHED SIZE

50 1/4" x 22 3/4"

FINISHED BLOCK SIZE

13 3/4" x 13 3/4"

MATERIALS

1 1/3 yd. multitonal fabric (the fabric used in the sample has colorways that graduate from light pink to dark rose, and light lilac to dark purple)

2 yd. black-on-black print (assumes borders are not pieced)

1 1/2 yd. backing fabric

Black thread

Batting

CUTTING

Multitonal fabric

- From the lengthwise grain of the fabric, cut 1 strip 14¼" wide. From this strip, cut 2 squares 14¼" x 14¼". These are the blocks on each side of the pieced center block.
- Cut the rest of the 14¼" strip into 1¾" strips. From the 1¾" strips, make the following subcuts:
- **A:** 9 squares 1¾" x 1¾"
- **B:** 2 strips 1¾" x 3"
- **C:** 2 strips 1¾" x 4¼"
- **D:** 2 strips 1¾" x 5½"
- **E:** 2 strips 1¾" x 6¾"
- From the lengthwise grain of the fabric, cut 2 strips 1¼" x 17½" and 2 strips 1¼" x 47½" (for narrow middle border)

Black-on-black print fabric

From the lengthwise grain of the fabric, cut

- 2 strips 2" x 14¼" (inner border, sides)
- 2 strips 2" x 45" (inner border, top and bottom)
- 2 strips 2¾" x 19½" (outer border, sides)
- 2 strips 2¾" x 51" (outer border, top and bottom)
- 3 strips 2⅛" by length of fabric (binding)
- From the lengthwise grain of the fabric, cut 2 strips 1¾" wide x length of fabric. From these strips, make the following subcuts:
- **F:** 14 squares 1¾" x 1¾"
- **G:** 2 strips 1¾" x 4¼"
- **H:** 2 strips 1¾" x 6¾"
- **I:** 2 strips 1¾" x 9¼"
- **J:** 2 strips 1¾" x 11¾"
- **K:** 2 strips 1¾" x 14¼"

CONSTRUCTION

MAKING THE CENTER BLOCK

The center block is made like a Courthouse Steps block. Beginning with a single center square, strips (sometimes black, sometimes black and multitonal pieced) are sewn first to the top and bottom, and then to each side. Then strips are added to that unit in the same way, first to the top and bottom, and then to each side. Refer to the block progression shown in the illustrations (Figs. 1–10) as a guide. Using the letters A–K from the cutting instructions, the following steps list the progression for sewing the pieces together. **Press after every step**, always pressing seam allowances away from the center square.

1. F-A-F
2. Sew G to each side of #1

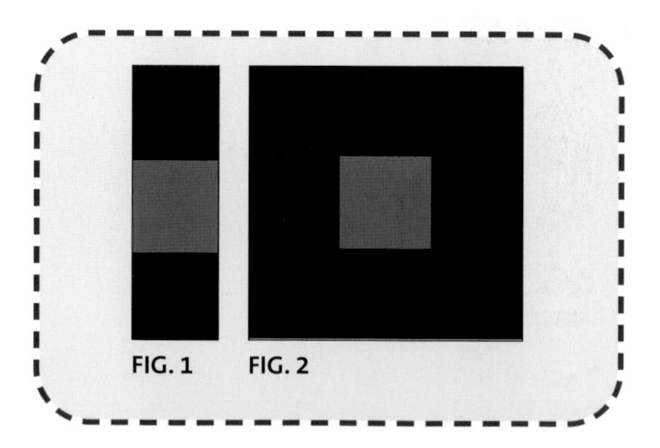

FIG. 1 FIG. 2

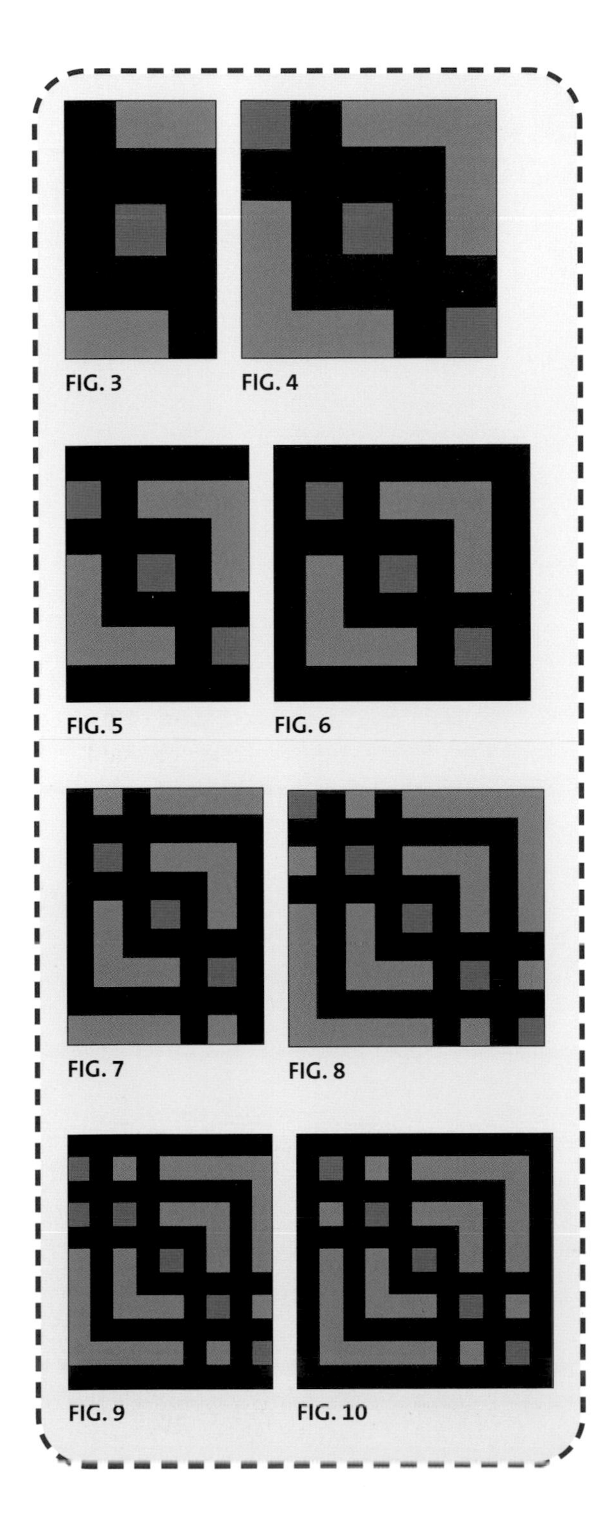

3. F-B (make 2); sew to top and bottom of #2
4. A-F-C (make 2); sew to sides of #3
5. Sew H to top and bottom of #4
6. Sew I to sides of #5
7. F-A-F-D (make 2); sew to top and bottom of #6
8. A-F-A-F-E (make 2); sew to sides of #7
9. Sew J to top and bottom of #8
10. Sew K to sides of #9

ASSEMBLING THE TABLE RUNNER

11. Square up the center block, if necessary. If your center block comes out smaller than 14 1/4" square, then trim the 14 1/4" squares of multitonal fabric to match. Sew one of the large squares of multitonal fabric to each side of the center block. Press seams toward the side blocks.
12. Sew one of the 2" x 14 1/4" black strips to each short side of the runner (trimming the strip, if necessary, to the same measurement as the short sides). Press seams away from center.
13. Measure the runner lengthwise through the center. Trim the black 45" strips to this measurement, and sew one strip to the top and one to the bottom of the runner. Press seams away from center.
14. Measure the width of the runner (the short measurement) through the center. Trim the 17 1/2" multitonal strips to this measurement, and sew one strip to each short side of the runner. Press seams away from center.

15. Measure the runner lengthwise through the center. Trim the $47\frac{1}{2}$" multitonal strips to this measurement, and sew one strip to the top and one to bottom of the runner. Press seams away from center.

16. Measure the width of the runner through the center. Trim the $19\frac{1}{2}$" black strips to this measurement, and sew one strip to each side of the runner. Press seams away from center.

17. Measure the runner lengthwise, through the center. Trim the 51" black strips to this measurement, and sew one strip to the top and one to the bottom of the runner. Press seams away from center.

18. Layer backing (wrong side up), batting, and top (right side up). Baste, and quilt as desired.

19. Add binding as described in First-Rate Bindings, on page 15.

the placemats

DESIGNER

Tomme J. Fent

FINISHED SIZE

$21\frac{3}{4}$" x $16\frac{3}{4}$"

FINISHED BLOCK SIZE

$13\frac{3}{4}$" x $13\frac{3}{4}$"

Fabric requirements are given for one placemat. Repeat as necessary for the number you need.

MATERIALS

$\frac{2}{3}$ yd. multitonal fabric (for top, narrow border, and backing)

$\frac{2}{3}$ yd. black-on-black print (assumes borders are not pieced)

Black thread

Batting

Difficulty:

CUTTING

Multitonal fabric

- From the lengthwise grain of the fabric, cut 3 strips $1\frac{3}{4}$" wide. From these strips, make the following subcuts:
- **A:** 9 squares $1\frac{3}{4}$" x $1\frac{3}{4}$"
- **B:** 2 strips $1\frac{3}{4}$" x 3"
- **C:** 2 strips $1\frac{3}{4}$" x $4\frac{1}{4}$"

- **D:** 2 strips $1^{3}/_{4}$" x $5^{1}/_{2}$"
- **E:** 2 strips $1^{3}/_{4}$" x $6^{3}/_{4}$"
- From the lengthwise grain of the fabric, cut 2 strips 1" x $15^{1}/_{2}$" and 2 strips 1" x $14^{1}/_{2}$" (for narrow border).

Black-on-black print fabric

- From the lengthwise grain of the fabric, cut 5 strips $1^{3}/_{4}$" wide. From these strips, make the following subcuts:
- **F:** 14 squares $1^{3}/_{4}$" x $1^{3}/_{4}$"
- **G:** 2 strips $1^{3}/_{4}$" x $4^{1}/_{4}$"
- **H:** 2 strips $1^{3}/_{4}$" x $6^{3}/_{4}$"
- **I:** 2 strips $1^{3}/_{4}$" x $9^{1}/_{4}$"
- **J:** 2 strips $1^{3}/_{4}$" x $11^{3}/_{4}$"
- **K:** 2 strips $1^{3}/_{4}$" x $14^{1}/_{4}$"
- From the lengthwise grain of the fabric, cut 2 strips 4" x 16" (side borders) and 2 strips $1^{1}/_{2}$" x 23" (top and bottom borders)
- From the lengthwise grain of the fabric, cut 3 strips $2^{1}/_{8}$" wide (binding).

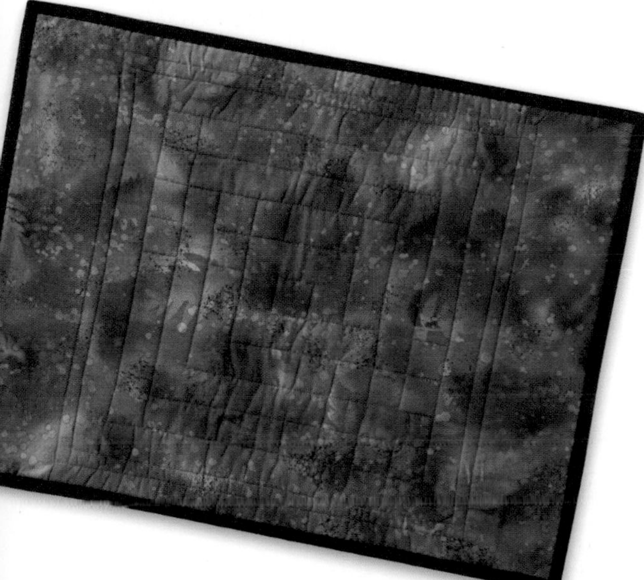

CONSTRUCTION

1. Make the center block as instructed in steps 1–10 for the table runner. Square up the block, if necessary.
2. Trim the two 1" x $14^{1}/_{2}$" multitonal strips to the same size as the center block, and sew one strip to each side of the center unit. Sew with the multitonal strip on top, and take care to sew an accurate $^{1}/_{4}$" from the edge of the strip. Press *toward* the center.
3. Measure the center unit from the outer edge of one multitonal strip to the outer edge of the other multitonal strip, and trim the two multitonal 1" x $15^{1}/_{2}$" strips to this measurement. Sew one of the strips to the top and one to the bottom of the center unit in the same manner as described in step 2. Press seams *toward* the center.
4. Measure the placemat from top to bottom, and trim the two 4" x 16" black strips to this measurement. Sew one strip to each side of the placemat. Press seams *away* from the center.
5. Measure the placemat from side to side through the center, and trim the two $1^{1}/_{2}$" x 23" black strips to this measurement. Sew one strip to the top and one to the bottom of the placemat. Press seams *away* from the center.
6. Layer backing (wrong side up), batting, and top (right side up). Baste, and quilt as desired.
7. Bind as described in First-Rate Bindings on page 15.

Dinner is served!

indigo nights quilt

INDIGO NIGHTS MADE BY TOMME J. FENT
QUILTED BY JAN GIBSON-KORYTKOWSKI

Light some incense, bring out the massage oil, and relax on this Asian-inspired beauty that features Japanese indigo fabrics and the *kanji* symbols for "calm" and "rest." The quilt is so easy to make that even a quilting novice can complete the project in a couple of days.

Difficulty: 

DESIGNER

Tomme J. Fent

FINISHED SIZE

91" x 103"

FINISHED BLOCK SIZE

30" x 36"

MATERIALS

2 yd. (total) assorted indigo prints for blocks

2 yd. beige fabric for appliqué background

1½ yd. dark blue fabric for narrow inner border (½ yd. if pieced)

2⅓ yd. blue-on-cream print for second border (1¼ yd. if pieced)

3 yd. of a single indigo fabric for outer border

2 yd. indigo fabrics for *kanji* appliqués

1 yd. of indigo fabric for binding

2 yd. lightweight fusible webbing

Thread to match beige background fabric

Monofilament thread

Dark gray thread for piecing

quilt wise

Having trouble finding just the right color of background fabric? Try looking at the *back* sides of fabrics! The beige fabric in the photo quilt is the back side of the fabric.

CUTTING

Important: Prewash all the fabrics for this quilt—the indigo fabrics to prevent bleeding in later washings, and the beige fabric so the fused appliqués will adhere well.

- From the assorted indigo prints, cut 60 squares 6½" x 6½".
- From the beige background fabric, cut 2 rectangles 31" x 37", and cut 1 rectangle 3" x 6" (we'll use this small rectangle to adjust your machine for appliquéing with monofilament thread).
- From the dark blue fabric, cut (or piece) 2 strips 2" x 74", and 2 strips 2" x 65".
- From the blue-on-cream fabric, cut (or piece) 2 strips 5" x 77", and 2 strips 5" x 74".
- From the single indigo print, cut 2 strips 10" x 93", and 2 strips 10" x 86", for outer border.

  do it right: To cut 10"-wide strips easily, use two 6"-wide rotary cutting rulers. Lay the 4" line from one ruler along the edge of the fabric, and place the second ruler alongside the first. Cut along the edge of the second ruler.

- From the indigo appliqué fabric, cut 2 rectangles approx. 30" x 34", and cut 1 strip 1" x 4" to use for setting up your machine to appliqué.
- From the fusible webbing, cut 2 rectangles approximately 29½" x 33½".
- From the binding fabric, cut 12 strips 2⅛" x length of fabric.

CONSTRUCTION

1. Take appliqué patterns to a copy shop and have them enlarged 600%. Cut around outside edges, smoothing curves as necessary to compensate for distortion that occurs during enlargement process.
2. Fuse webbing rectangles to wrong side of 30" x 34" indigo appliqué fabric rectangles per manufacturer's instructions. Next, fold the fabric in half lengthwise and widthwise, and finger press lightly, just enough so you can see the creases.

calm

rest

3. Pin appliqué patterns onto the front of indigo appliqué fabric that has been prepared with fusible webbing. Cut around outside edges.
4. Using the pressed creases and the original appliqué patterns as guides, center the appliqués on the right side of the background rectangles, and fuse per manufacturer's instructions.
5. Thread your sewing machine with monofilament thread in the top, and thread to match the beige background fabric in the bobbin. Center the 1" x 4" strip of appliqué fabric on top of the 3" x 6" rectangle of beige background fabric. Set your machine for a short, narrow zigzag stitch (1.5-mm long x 2.5-mm wide). Stitch down one side of the indigo strip, making sure the left-hand swing of the zigzag stitch catches the indigo and the right-hand swing of the zigzag falls on the background fabric. Use this practice piece as a guide to check the tension on your machine. Most machines require you to reduce the top tension, sometimes quite a lot, when using monofilament thread in the top. If you can see the beige bobbin thread peeking through on the indigo fabric, reduce your top tension and stitch more. Keep reducing top tension until you can no longer see bobbin thread peeking through, but not so much that your stitch loses its integrity. Now you are ready to appliqué around the *kanji* symbols.

quilt wise

When you finish the machine appliqué, you may still have a tiny point or two where the bobbin thread shows on the dark indigo fabric. Touch up these points with a permanent black fabric marker. You'll be the only person who knows!

6. Stitch around the entire outside edge of each appliqué using a narrow, short zigzag stitch (1.5-mm long x 2.5-mm wide).
7. Trim the appliqué blocks to 30½" x 36½".
8. Change to dark gray thread in top and bobbin. Join the 6½" indigo squares in random order, making 6 rows with 5 squares in each row. Lay out the rows and rearrange until you're satisfied with the placement. Then press rows 1, 3, and 5 with seam allowances going to the right, and rows 2, 4, and 6 with seam allowances going to the left. Join the rows, matching the seams between the squares. Repeat these steps to make a second block of 30 squares.
9. Join one of the blocks of indigo squares to the right side of the appliqué block containing the *kanji* symbol for "calm." Join the other block of indigo squares to the left side of the appliqué block containing the *kanji* symbol for "rest." Press seams toward the indigo blocks.

10. Join the two rows, as shown in the photo quilt. Press seam allowance to one side.
11. Measure the length of the quilt through the center, and trim the 2" x 74" dark blue strips to this length. Attach one of the strips to each side of the quilt. Press seam allowances toward the dark blue strips.
12. Measure the width of the quilt through the center, and trim the 2" x 65" dark blue strips to this length. Attach one of the strips to the top and one to the bottom of the quilt. Press seam allowances toward the dark blue strips.
13. Measure the length of the quilt through the center, and trim the 5" x 77" blue-on-cream strips to this length. Attach one of the strips to each side of the quilt. Press seam allowances *toward the dark blue strip*. (Having both seams pressed toward this small inner border will emphasize the border when the quilt is quilted.)
14. Measure the width of the quilt through the center, and trim the 5" x 74" dark blue strips to this length. Attach one of the strips to the top and one to the bottom of the quilt. Press seam allowances toward the dark blue strips.
15. Measure the length of the quilt through the center, and trim the 10" x 86" indigo strips to this length. Attach one of the strips to each side of the quilt. Press seam allowances toward the indigo border.
16. Measure the width of the quilt through the center, and trim the 10" x 93" indigo strips to this length. Attach one of the strips to the top and one to the bottom of the quilt. Press seam allowances toward the indigo border.
17. Piece together fabric to make a backing that is at least 95" x 107". (See photo below.) Layer backing, batting, and quilt top, and quilt as desired. (The photo quilt used echo quilting around the *kanji* symbols, and traditional Japanese designs in the indigo blocks and borders.)
18. Make binding as instructed in First-Rate Bindings on page 15.
19. Add a label. Wash and dry the quilt to emphasize the quilting. Sweet dreams!

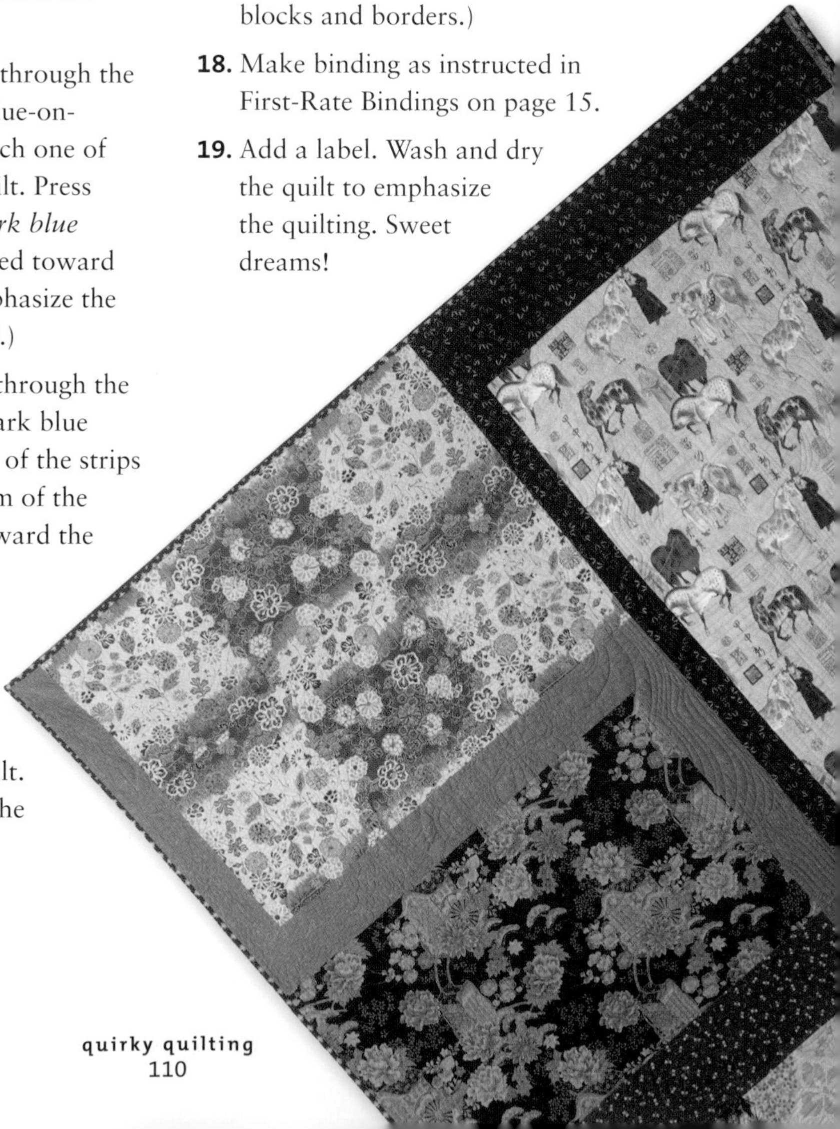

mum's the word wall hanging

The calm beauty of Japanese art is reflected in this wall hanging, which invites you to remember springtime and the scent of flowers. Fabric paints or pastels, a reusable stamp you can make yourself, and a touch of bamboo for hanging make up this creative project, which would look right at home on the wall next to the Indigo Nights Quilt.

Difficulty:

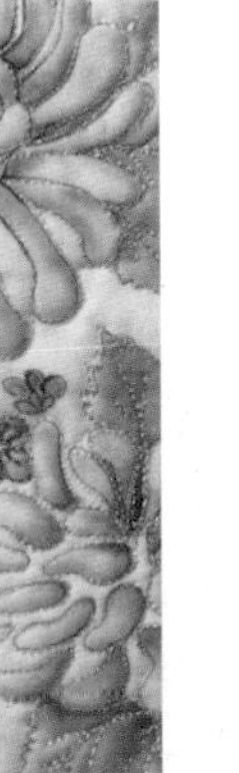

DESIGNER

Val Deane Osmers

FINISHED SIZE

$12\frac{1}{4}$" x $18\frac{1}{2}$"

MATERIALS

$\frac{1}{2}$ yd. unbleached muslin or other light fabric for front and back

$\frac{1}{4}$ yd. print fabric for borders

13" x 19" piece of low-loft batting

Cork or Fun Foam™ for stamp

Fabric paints or D'UVA ChromaCoal Heat Fixable Pastels®

Fabric markers

6" machine embroidery hoop

Embroidery threads

16" piece of bamboo, dowel, or other rod for hanging

Approx. 22" of cord for hanging

CUTTING

From muslin:

- 1 rectangle 13" x 23" for top
- 1 rectangle 13" x 19" for backing
- 1 rectangle 10½" x 3" for hanging sleeve
- From border fabric, cut two strips 3½" x width of fabric.

PAINTING ON FABRIC

There are many different brands of textile paints, inks, and markers on the market today that can be heat set for permanency. The mums in this project were painted with D'UVA ChromaCoal Heat Fixable Pastels®. These come in a dry stick form, 10 colors to a set, and other colors can be created by blending directly on the fabric. They are very portable, create little mess, and can be erased or removed with water until they are heat set. Additional applications of color following heat setting will intensify the colors without changing the hand, or feel, of the fabric.

Cotton swabs sold in the eye makeup section of your local pharmacy are inexpensive and effective applicators. Look for swabs that have a firm point at one end and are somewhat flat and round on the opposite end. For applicators that last longer, look for Tsukineko Fantastix™ Coloring Tools, available through art supply stores and online sources.

To use the pastels, load a cotton swab with chalk by rubbing it on the end of the stick. **Caution:** Do not peel back the paper, which will cause the chalk to crumble! Brush off the excess on a paper towel until you become familiar with the process. Apply color to the fabric lightly, building up colors and layers. When you want an applied color to remain, heat set with an iron. Repeat the process to add additional colors, or to intensify a color.

In the alternative, you can use colored fabric markers or other forms of fabric paint to color the design, following the manufacturer's instructions.

PAINTING THE DESIGN

1. Copy the pattern on page 112 at 200%. Transfer the mum design (but not the Japanese *kanji* symbols) to the 13" x 23" muslin rectangle by tracing the pattern over a light box or on a window.
2. Referring to the directions above for painting on fabric, apply color to the background design, as follows. (Note: Before applying color to your design, try blending colors on a scrap of the fabric you are using. Colors may look different when applied to different fabrics.)

   Paint the mums with orange and yellow. Add highlights with violet and a touch of red.

   Paint the leaves with green, yellow at the tips, and violet for the shadows, and then add a light layer of charcoal to tone down the brightness.

   Paint the plum blossoms with violet and blue.
3. To add depth and form, outline images sparingly with fabric markers.

MAKING THE STAMP

1. Copy the *kanji* characters at 200%. Cut out characters around outside edge. Place cut-out characters *upside down* (to reverse) on cork or Fun Foam™, and trace around the reversed characters. Cut out the characters using scissors.
2. Glue the characters to a jar lid, piece of tile, small piece of wood, or other material that you can hold onto while stamping. *Be sure the character is still reversed:* the "wrong" side of the character should be faceup on the base. Allow glue to dry thoroughly.
3. Apply an even, thin layer of fabric paint to the stamp. (As an alternative, you can use a stamp pad with fabric-safe ink, such as VersaCraft™, formerly called Fabrico, inks.) If fabric paint is too thick or more translucency is desired, thin the paints with 100% aloe vera gel.
4. Place fabric on a layer of thin batting or felt rather than a hard surface and stamp images onto fabric, making sure you press down evenly over the design. Allow ink to dry.

ADDING DIMENSION

To emphasize the mums, add trapunto to the three larger flowers, as follows: Layer thin batting or felt under the three large flowers. Hoop each flower and sew around the petals using embroidery thread and a free-motion stitch, taking a backstitch at the beginning and end where the threads will be cut. This will anchor the stitches and prevent them from coming unsewn. Cut away the batting close to the stitching line.

睦

quilt wise

For free-motion stitching, use your machine's darning or free-motion foot, or if you don't have one, remove the foot altogether. Lower or cover the feed dogs, and reduce the top tension. You will be moving the fabric, rather than having the machine pull the fabric through. Practice this method on a small quilt sandwich (two layers of fabric with batting in between), if you have not done this before. Most sewing machine manuals and many quilting books have detailed explanations of how to do free-motion stitching.

CONSTRUCTION

ASSEMBLING THE CENTER

1. Make a quilt sandwich with the backing fabric on the bottom (wrong side up), batting in the middle, and painted fabric on top (right side up). The top should extend 2" beyond the backing and batting on the top and bottom. Center each design in the embroidery hoop and stitch around the flowers, loosely following the flower shape, using an embroidery thread a bit darker or lighter than the flower. A slightly contrasting thread color will enhance the overall effect. Repeat the same technique to stitch around the leaves and plum blossoms. Press.
2. Trim the sides to be sure they are straight and even. Press under 1/2" of the painted fabric on the top and bottom edges. Then fold the excess flap of fabric over to the back side of the quilt and press. Hand stitch the folded-over fabric to the back side of the quilt.
3. Make a rod pocket or sleeve as follows. Fold in 1/4" on each end of the 10 1/2" x 3" strip of fabric and press. Fold in another 1/4" and machine stitch in place, close to the first fold. Fold the strip in half lengthwise (so it's now 1 1/2" wide), wrong sides together. Stitch long raw edge using a 1/4" seam. Press seam to one side. Press the tube so the long seam is in the center, on the back side of the tube.

   Center the rod pocket on the upper back of the quilt, on the fabric flap that was folded over from the front. Hand stitch the tube to the quilt along the top and bottom edges, leaving the sides open.

ADDING THE SIDE BORDERS

1. Fold the 3 1/2" strips of border fabric in half lengthwise, wrong sides together, and press a sharp crease. Begin turning under 1/2" on one long edge of the strip, and run the strip under the presser foot, sewing *without thread*, using the presser foot as a guide. This will give you a straight, pressed, turned edge without burned fingers from trying to turn under an even edge with an iron. Repeat on the other long edge of the strip, but this time turning under a 1/4" to 3/8" edge. Follow the same procedure with the other strip. *Do not trim the strips* at this point.
2. Lay the quilt facedown. Place the border strip on top of the quilt, right side up, with the narrower pressed edge toward the

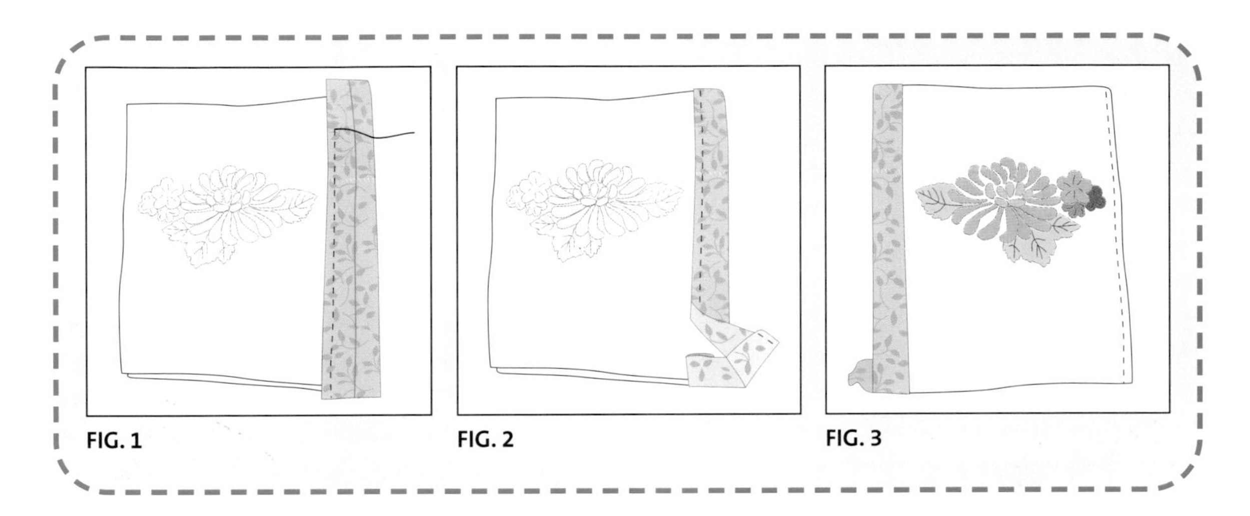

quilt's center, and the raw edge of the quilt lined up against the pressed crease in the center of the border strip. (Fig. 1) You're not wrapping the whole border strip around the quilt at this point; you're only positioning the side of the border strip with the narrower pressed edge on the back of the quilt. The quilt should be centered between the long tails on each end of the border strip, and the narrow pressed edge of the border strip should be toward the center of the quilt. Using a basting or long stitch on your machine, baste approximately 1/4" from the pressed-under edge, stitching through the entire quilt sandwich, and stopping about 3/4" from each end. This will help the border stay straight and even as you sew it on. Break or snip the basting stitches every couple of inches to release any possible ripples or pulls. (If you don't clip the threads, the reason for clipping will be apparent when you try to stitch the border to the quilt!) Press, making sure the border is flat.

3. Trim the top and bottom of each border strip so it extends 1/4" to 5/8" past the top and bottom of the quilt. Fold the excess to the underside of the border strip at the top and bottom, making the edges even with the top and bottom of the quilt. (Fig. 2) Press.
4. Turn the quilt over. Bring the border strips around to the front of the quilt and pin. (Fig. 3) Make sure the top and bottom edges of the border strip are even. Each border strip should be the same width on the front and back of the quilt. Stitch close to the front edge of the border strip. If the borders have been folded and pressed properly, you will be stitching through both layers of the border fabric, with the quilt sandwiched neatly inside the border strip. Remove the basting stitches.
5. Slip stitch the top and bottom of the border strips closed for a clean finish.
6. Insert the bamboo or other rod through the hanging sleeve. Attach a length of cord to each end, and hang your quilt.

amazed wall hanging

MADE BY TOMME J. FENT, QUILTED BY JAN GIBSON-KORYTKOWSKI

A quilted wall hanging can be a stylish alternative to a painting or print for decorating your home or office. The Scotch Plaid block used in this wall hanging offers infinite design possibilities. Depending on where you locate the various fabrics and colors, the maze effect created by the black fabric can assume a wide variety of shapes. A computer design program such as EQ5 will allow you to try dozens of possible combinations.

Difficulty:

DESIGNER

Tomme J. Fent

FINISHED SIZE

49" x 49"

FINISHED BLOCK SIZE

7½" x 7½"

NOTES ON FABRIC SELECTION

Values (light, medium, dark) are more important than color in designing this quilt. One way to choose fabrics is to start with a large-scale, multicolored floral, and then select fabrics to coordinate with it. The photo quilt followed this method. The floral fabric includes greens from light gray-green to teal, pinks and reds, brown, blue, and purple. The coordinating fabrics include a teal tone-on-tone floral, a mottled green, a gray-green leafy print, a brown leafy print, a red stripe, a mottled pink, and a mottled blue. The background fabric is off-white with faint red motifs.

Rather than trying to match the fabrics in the photo quilt, which would be difficult to impossible, concentrate on finding values similar to those used in the quilt. We've given you fabric requirements and diagrams to show the distribution of each different value in the quilt.

FIG. 1

FIG. 2

MATERIALS

⅔ yd. **background fabric,** shown as white in all the figures

2 yd. **solid black fabric** (assumes borders are not pieced)

Fig. 1 shows where the black goes in the quilt. In the photo quilt, an occasional mottled green is substituted for the black.

1 yd. **large-scale floral fabric**

The red triangles in Fig. 2 show where the floral goes in the quilt.

1¼ yd. (total) of **medium-value, coordinating fabrics**

The blue triangles in Fig. 3 show where the medium-value fabrics go in the quilt. In the photo of the quilt, these are the stripe, mottled pink, and gray-green leafy print.

1¼ yd. (total) of **dark-value, coordinating fabrics**

The tan triangles in Fig. 4 show where the dark-value fabrics go in the quilt. In the photo of the quilt, these are the mottled blue, teal-on-teal print, brown leafy print, and mottled green.

FIG. 3

FIG. 4

CUTTING

Unlike with many quilts made from half-square triangles, there is no quick way to speed piece this quilt by making triangles from squares. You actually have to cut triangles and then piece them together. However, this also allows you a great deal of freedom in designing your quilt. Play with the design using a design wall, EQ5, or even colored triangles cut from construction paper. You can use the design shown in the photo, or rearrange the triangles to come up with your own design.

Background fabric:

- Cut 37 squares 3½" x 3½". Cut each square in half on the diagonal to make 74 triangles.

Black fabric:

- From lengthwise grain of fabric, cut 4 strips 2½" x 54" (borders).
- From lengthwise grain of fabric, cut 4 strips 2⅛" x 50" (binding).
- Cut 76 squares 3½" x 3½". Cut each square in half on the diagonal to make 152 triangles.

Large-scale floral fabric:

- 17 squares 6" x 6". Cut each square in half on the diagonal to make 33 triangles (you will have one extra).

Medium-value fabrics:

- 33 (total) squares 3½" x 3½" and 8 squares 6" x 6". Cut each square in half on the diagonal to make 81 triangles (65 small and 16 large, with 1 small left over).

Note: The photo quilt has large triangles—5 of mottled pink, 11 of red stripe; small triangles—7 mottled pink, 58 gray-green leafy print.

Dark-value fabrics:

- 37 (total) squares 3½" x 3½" and 12 squares 6" x 6". Cut each square in half on the diagonal to make 96 triangles (73 small and 23 large, with 1 large and 1 small left over).

Note: The photo quilt has large triangles—17 dark blue, 6 teal-on-teal print; small triangles—8 dark blue, 18 teal-on-teal print, 25 brown leafy print, 22 mottled green.

quilt wise

Having even a small design wall makes designing quilts an enjoyable pastime. There are a number of methods you can use to make a design wall. If you have a large section of wall available, consider covering the wall with cork, and then pinning or stapling a flannel design wall to the cork. For a more movable design wall, try covering a large piece of foam core board with white flannel. For a very portable design wall, the flannel backs of vinyl tablecloths work well. If you share your sewing space with other household activities, you can even fuse white flannel to the inside of a window shade for a pull-down design wall that can be rolled up with blocks still on it!

CONSTRUCTION

PIECING THE BLOCKS

Every block in the quilt is made the same way, and then the blocks are set 6 across and 6 down, with borders added as the last step.

Each Scotch Plaid block is made up of 10 small triangles and 2 large triangles, sewn together as shown in Fig. 5. The easiest way to assemble the blocks, and then the quilt, is to lay out all the triangles and rearrange them until you're satisfied with the arrangement. Then transfer the triangles, one full block at a time, to a piece of cardboard or small cutting board to carry the block to your machine. Assemble the block exactly as you have it laid out, pressing as you go, and then return the block to its place in the layout and move on to the next block. This will keep the triangles in position, and your black maze will end up looking like you designed it. **Note:** If one of your fabrics is a stripe, take care to turn the triangles so the stripes are all going in the same direction (either horizontal or vertical).

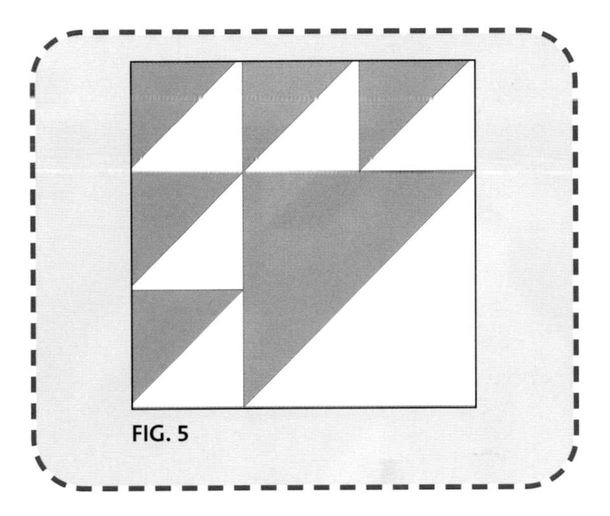

FIG. 5

quilt wise

Be careful when handling and sewing triangles. The bias edges will stretch and distort easily. If you do not have a single-needle throat plate for your sewing machine (a throat plate with a single, small hole for the needle to enter, instead of the wider hole used for zigzag stitching), you can make a temporary one by using an old sewing machine needle and poking a hole through a 3" x 5" index card. Wiggle the needle around to enlarge the hole just a bit. Then place the card under the needle on your machine, and slowly lower the needle through the hole by hand. Tape the card in place on the bed of your sewing machine. Using a single-needle throat plate will help prevent the corners of the triangles from getting pushed down into your machine as you begin stitching. Also, use the chain-piecing method described in Join the Chain Gang on page 10.

ASSEMBLING THE QUILT

When all blocks are assembled, sew them into rows. Press seam allowances in rows 1, 3, and 5 to the right, and in rows 2, 4, and 6 to the left, and then join the rows, matching the seams. (See photo quilt, page 120.) Press the quilt.

Measure the length of the quilt through the center. Cut two of the black border strips to this measurement, and attach one to each side of the quilt.

Measure the width of the quilt through the center. Cut the remaining two black border strips to this measurement, and attach one to the top and one to the bottom of the quilt.

Layer backing (wrong side up), batting, and quilt top (right side up), and quilt as desired. Add binding as described in First-Rate Bindings on page 15, and label your quilt. To hang your quilt, attach a hanging sleeve as described in Be a Show-off on page 17.

APPENDIX

acknowledgments

It's time to introduce and acknowledge the members of "the band," without whom this book would not have been possible. My heartfelt thanks go out to the following:

On lead guitar, the great designers who stepped up to contribute such wonderful, fun, quirky patterns to this book: Zelma Abbott, Ann Brouillette, Janice Cook, Nina Gilliland, Margaret Hunt, Val Deane Osmers, Sophia Snider, Eithne Taaffe, and Jane Vereen.

On rhythm guitar, the Quirk Packaging team—Sharyn, Sarah, Lynne, Sue, and Peg—who pulled together my jumble of numbers, words, and drawings to create this delightful book!

On bass, all the quilters in my life, past and present. Your quilts amaze and inspire me, your friendship and support keep me going, and your confidence in me keeps me humble and grateful.

On drums (making the most noise!), my "cheering section," in writing this book and elsewhere: Craig, Bun & Buck, Ernie, Michael, Larry, Carrie, Ginny, Jaime, John, Judy & John & that other John(ny), Jeff & Vicki, Jim & Karen, Frann, Lynn & Cloyann, Gary, Lerlene, Sygne, Sharon, Leslie, Paul, Fred, Clay, Dwight & Darla, Melisa, and the "heavenly choir"—Mom, Dad, Grandma & Grandpa, MeMaw & PaPaw, Richard, Aunt Mary Ellen & Uncle Charlie, and Janice.

And finally, the "roadies," who have kept me sane and given me so much love and companionship: Max, the "Devil Dog"; the Little Peeps; Wicket, the "Flame Dog"; and Tater, the "Little Tot."

meet the designers

Zelma Abbott of Sioux City, Iowa, grew up surrounded by quilts-in-progress, where she literally played beneath the ever-changing patterned quilts made by her Grandma Lusher's Community Club members. Zelma made her first quilt (which was tied) at age nineteen. The quilt featured a textile-painted Zodiac symbol that was made using an iron-on transfer pattern from a magazine. The seeds of a "quiltaholic" were sewn but lay dormant for several years until a back injury forced Zelma to take up an activity less strenuous than reupholstery. When she took a hand quilting class at a local community college, quilting took center stage. As a professional hand quilter and maker of wearable art, quilting is truly Zelma's life. Contact Zelma at stitcz4u@cableone.net.

Ann Brouillette lives in Sioux City, Iowa, with her husband, Scott, and three sons—Dan, Zac, and Eric. She has been sewing for about thirty-eight years, and quilting for the last twenty-five. Ann is the owner of Heart & Hand Dry Goods Company in Sioux City, which was featured as one of the Top 10 Quilt Shops in the 1999 issue of the *Better Homes & Gardens* "Quilt Sampler." She has been designing a pillow-of-the-month for the shop for the last seven years. Contact Ann at Heart & Hand Dry Goods Co. (see Resources, page 124), or threadhead1@aol.com.

Janice Cook became interested in quilting thirty years ago after inheriting several fifty-year-old quilt tops made by her husband's great grandmother. Soon she began a lifelong quest to learn how to finish the treasured quilt tops. Janice lives in South Dakota with her husband and three sons. She continues to explore all realms of quiltmaking for herself, her family, and future generations. Contact Janice at cookiejrn@aol.com.

Nina Gilliland remembers, as a child, watching her maternal grandparents quilting around a handmade wooden frame. This was when her love of quilts began, but it wasn't until much later, after years of sewing clothing for herself and her daughters, that Nina was introduced to quilting by her sister Tomme (the author of this book). Currently, Nina is a secretary for a private university where she is working on her bachelor's degree in English. She has been married to her husband, Buck, for thirty years, and is the mother of three daughters, "American mom" to a host of international exchange students, and grandmother to Tessa and Ian. Nina's favorite vacation is spending a week at sister Tomme's Iowa home, where the two of them quilt until the wee hours, enjoy the gourmet cooking of Tomme's husband, Craig, and laugh themselves silly. Contact Nina at okquiltluvr@yahoo.com.

Margaret Hunt, known to family and friends as "Maggie," makes her home in Clarks Hill, South Carolina, on the banks of the lovely Savannah River. Maggie lives with her husband, sons, and two Jack Russell terriers, Charlie and Jazz, who personally test all of her quilts. A quiltmaker for more than thirty years, Maggie got her first blue ribbon in the fourth grade for a 4H apron project, and she's never looked back. She recently was honored to have nine of her "Journal Quilts" acquired by Quilts, Inc., the parent company of the International Quilt Festival, for its corporate collection. Maggie's friends swear she never sleeps because she produces so many quilts and wearables, but she says she's just a "speed demon" at the sewing machine. Contact Maggie at mchunt@wctel.net, and see more of her work at www.theartquilt.com/mchunt.

Val Deane Osmers lives in San Diego, California, with her husband, two dogs, a cat, and four betas. She began painting on fabric as a child (not always with parental approval), and started doing free-motion embroidery or "thread painting" shortly after college. A non-creative career and a tendency to be a "perpetual student" led Val Deane to take numerous seminars and classes in textile art, and her focus ultimately evolved into making art quilts. Contact her at bodeanedesigns@yahoo.com.

Sophia Snider has been sewing since she was five years old. She always wanted to learn how to quilt, but just didn't find it feasible while living in a small house. One Saturday morning, she happened upon the PBS show "Lap Quilting with Georgia Bonesteel." She bought the companion book and the rest is history. Lately, Sophia's quilting inspiration has come from her three young grandchildren. She lives in Oklahoma City, Oklahoma, with her husband, John, and their Yorkshire Terrier, DeLancie. Contact Sophia at P.O. Box 55778, Del City, OK 73155, or sofyann@cox.net.

Eithne Taaffe has been fascinated by quilting for a very long time, but it wasn't until she fell in love with a quilt featured in a magazine that she became determined to learn the craft. She enrolled in a quilting class in midtown Manhattan and was surprised to find it was being taught by the designer of the quilt that had inspired her! Like lightning, she became addicted to the art of quilting. She enjoys a variety of interests including fencing, travel, theater, politics, flying, and more; quilting allows her to incorporate many of those themes into her designs. Eithne lives and works in New York City, where she spends way too much time playing with fabric and designing funky, whimsical quilts. To see some of Eithne's work, visit her website at www.taibhse.com.

Jane Vereen has been quilting for over twenty years and loves everything about it! She teaches quilting classes at Heart & Hand Dry Goods Company, a quilt shop in Sioux City, Iowa. Jane, who is a trained musician and music educator, says the process of creating beautiful quilts has opened up a creative outlet that feeds her soul. She lives in Sioux City with her husband and three children. Contact Jane at Heart & Hand Dry Goods Co. (see Resources, page 124).

resources

The author and designers suggest you check with your local quilt shops first for the products and materials referenced in this book. If you can't find what you need locally, then we recommend the following sources.

BEAR THREAD DESIGNS

(Home of the Appliqué Pressing Sheet)
P.O. Box 1452
Highland, TX 77562
1-281-462-0661
www.bearthreaddesigns.com

BIG HORN QUILTS

(Full-service quilt shop with fabric, notions, books, and more)
529 Greybull Avenue
P.O. Box 566
Greybull, WY 82426
Toll free: 1-877-586-9150
Outside the U.S.: 1-307-765-2604
www.bighornquilts.com

CARYL BRYER FALLERT

(Bubble Jet Set 2000®, related products, and tips)
Bryerpatch Studio
P.O. Box 945
Oswego, IL 60543
www.bryerpatch.com

CITY QUILTER

(Sophisticated, exotic fabric for the urban quilter)
133 West 25th Street
New York, NY 10001
1-212-807-9451
www.cityquilter.com

DICK BLICK

(D'UVA ChromaCoal Heat Fixable Pastels)
P.O. Box 1267
Galesburg, IL 61402-1267
Toll free: 1-800-447-8192
www.dickblick.com

THE ELECTRIC QUILT COMPANY

419 Gould Street, Suite 2
Bowling Green, OH 43402
Toll free: 1-800-356-4219
www.electricquilt.com

GOODWILL INDUSTRIES

(Great source for wide neckties and clothing made from unique fabrics)
1-301-530-6500
http://locator.goodwill.org

HEART & HAND DRY GOODS CO.

(Full-service quilt shop that sells most items used in these patterns, including Timtex, Appliqué Pressing Sheet, and brushed cotton plaids)
1551 Indian Hills Drive, #6
Sioux City, IA 51104
1-712-258-3161
www.heartandhand.com

HOBBY LOBBY

(Threads, beaded fringe by the yard, iron-on appliqués, and more)
Stores throughout central and southeastern U.S.
1-615-373-1444
www.hobbylobby.com

JERRY'S ARTARAMA

(D'UVA ChromaCoal Heat Fixable Pastels)
5325 Departure Drive
Raleigh, NC 27616
Toll free: 1-800-U-Artist (827-8478)
www.jerrysartarama.com

LONG CREEK MILLS

(Great prices on glitzy beads)

802 Bessemer City Road
Gastonia, NC 28052
1-704-864-6651
www.LongCreekMills.com

LOVING STITCHES

(Fine Fuse Fusible Adhesive)

150 Andrews Road
Fayetteville, NC 28311
1-910-630-3912
www.LovingStitches.net

MARY JO'S CLOTH STORE, INC.

(Fabric, notions, patterns, and trims)

I-85 Exit 21
401 Cox Road – Gaston Mall
Gastonia, NC 28054
Toll free: 1-800-MARY JO'S (1-800-627-9567)
www.maryjos.com

MY QUILT SHOP

(WaveEdge Ruler, Add-a-Quarter Ruler, ThimblePads, and all things "quilty")

206 First Street
Sergeant Bluff, IA 51054
1-712-943-9486
www.kimsquilts.com

PATCHWORK PENGUIN

(Fabrics, yarn, patterns, notions, and more)

6450 Foothill Road
Suite B104
Tujunga, CA 91042
1-818-352-7300
www.patchworkpenguin.com

QUILT BUS

(Fine Fuse Fusible Adhesive, Appliqué Pressing Sheet)

www.quiltbus.com

QUILTER'S NOOK, INC.

(Machine quilting)

Elaine Kosnac
4038 Victory Blvd.
Staten Island, NY
1-718-494-8611
www.geocities.com/quiltersnook

SALVATION ARMY OUTLET STORES

(Great source for wide neckties and clothing made from unique fabrics)

www.redshield.org

THIMBLES BY T. J. LANE

(Thimbles)

P.O. Box 30595
Lincoln, NE 68503-0595
1-402-477-5222
www.Thimbles2fit.com

THE VIRGINIA QUILTER

(Fine Fuse Fusible Adhesive, Bubble Jet Set 2000®)

P.O. Box 83
Fredericksburg, VA 22404
Toll free: 1-866-827-8458 (VA QUILT)
Local: 1-540-548-3207
www.virginiaquilter.com

WAECHTER'S SILK SHOP

(Natural fiber fabric, buttons, fabric paints, and more)

94 Charlotte Street
Asheville, NC 28801
1-828-252-2131
www.fabricsandbuttons.com

index

Italic page numbers refer to illustrations.

meet the author

Tomme J. Fent was exposed to quilting almost from birth, as her maternal grandparents were both avid quilters. She recalls playing with her younger sister underneath the large quilting frame where her grandparents and some of their friends would sit and quilt all day. When dinnertime came around, the women retired to the kitchen to prepare the meal, while the men continued to quilt and discuss current events. Spending the night at Grandma's house always meant sleeping under a handmade quilt.

Although Tomme began sewing when she was little more than a toddler, she only started quilting in 1998, after a chance visit to a quilt shop in Norman, Oklahoma. In 1999, her first quilt, "This Is My Country," was shown in the American Quilter's Society show in Paducah, Kentucky, and in "Quilter's Newsletter Magazine." She loves all kinds of quilts, from traditional to quirky, and recently has begun focusing her energies on art quilts.

Tomme works as a lawyer to support her quilting habit. She lives in Sioux City, Iowa, with her husband, Craig, a ceramic artist, and their dog Max. Visit Tomme's website at http://community.webshots.com/user/tommequilts to see some of her quilts.

meet the photographer

Bill Milne is a photographer and image maker who's contributed to *Gourmet,* the *Wine Spectator, Time, People,* and many other publications. His clients range from Kraft Foods, Smirnoff, and Snapple to AT&T, Apple Computers, and Johnson & Johnson. Over the past 12 years, he's expanded into the areas of digital imaging, electronic composition, and retouching. He has also photographed more than 20 books, including *Halloween Parties* and *Knit Wit* (both Quirk Packaging).

meet the illustrator

Erica Mulherin is a self-taught artist, illustrator, and serial crafter whose illustrations also appear in *Knit Wit: 30 Easy and Hip Projects* (Quirk Packaging). In her life and work, Erica is influenced by artists such as Sergio Aragones, Berkeley Breathed, Maurice Sendak, Aubrey Beardsley, and Kay Nielsen. Erica was born and raised in Rawlins, Wyoming, and currently makes her home in Olympia, Washington.